CHOOSING TO LEAVE

Voluntary Retirement from the U.S. House of Representatives

John R. Hibbing
University of Nebraska-Lincoln

UNIVERSITY
PRESS OF
AMERICA

Library of Congress Catalog Card Number: 81-40635

To Mom and Dad

With much appreciation

ACKNOWLEDGEMENTS

Some of the material in this study is based upon work supported by the National Science Foundation under grant number SES-80-05138. In addition, some of the data utilized (mostly in Chapter 1) were made available by the Inter-university Consortium for Political and Social Research. The data were originally collected by Carroll R. McKibbin. Any opinions, findings, conclusions, or recommendations expressed herein do not necessarily reflect the views of the National Science Foundation, the Consortium, or Professor McKibbin. It should also be noted that Chapter 2 is a revised version of a study which appeared in the February 1982 issue of the Legislative Studies Quarterly. A somewhat altered version of Chapter 3 was presented at the 1981 meeting of the American Political Science Association in New York and will be appearing in the August 1982 issue of the American Journal of Political Science.

I am indebted to numerous individuals for their contributions to this study. Most of the former members of the U.S. House who voluntarily retired in 1978 gave very generously of their time and made important contributions to this study. Jacci Leger did a wonderful job of putting the manuscript in final form. Vernon and Ardyth Hibbing, to whom this work is dedicated, have been constant sources of support. Valuable advice at various stages of this project was rendered by John Alford, Gary Copeland, Richard Fenno, and especially Samuel C. Patterson -- whose comments on an earlier version were particularly beneficial. My wife, Anne Nielsen Hibbing, collected much of the data and contributed in innumerable other ways to this study. My heartfelt thanks to them all.

John R. Hibbing
Lincoln, Nebraska

TABLE OF CONTENTS

LIST OF TABLES

LIST OF FIGURES

INTRODUCTION

In 1968 a dozen members of the United States House of Representatives decided they would not seek re-election to that prestigious body or to any other public office. This situation is not startling. With 435 members, it is only natural that every two years a small number of elderly, enfeebled, homesick, or scandal-plagued members would pass the baton to younger, more vigorous, new members. Nor is the number of retirees in 1968 atypical of other election years in the 1960s; similarly small groups retired in 1962, 1964, 1966, and 1970.

However, ten years later, in 1978, the retiring class was not composed of just twelve members, but over two and one-half times that many -- 31. It was not composed of moss-back, out-of-step curmedgeons, but, for the most part, of energetic and imaginative legislators -- some of them proven over the course of several years but a surprising number with promising careers still before them. Again the selection of years is not misleading. The retiring classes in 1972, 1974, 1976, and 1980 included approximately 30 members.

Unlike 1968, the situation in 1978 is rather startling when put in historical context. Large numbers of voluntary retirements from the House were the norm in the nineteenth-century -- when service in a part-time and occasionally dangerous (see Polsby, 1968;166-67) body was, quite understandably, far from universally desired. But as the twentieth-century progressed the House lost most of the elements responsible for the high voluntary retirement rate of the 1800s. It became more stable and acquired more prestige, dignity and clout, the job gradually became full-time with corresponding adjustments in salary, and the conduct of members became much more professional. Given these improvements, it takes only a small amount of common sense reasoning to anticipate diminished and diminishing numbers of retirees from the twentieth-century House. This reasoning was borne out in the findings of many students of the 1950s-1960s House. Richard Wittmer (1964), Nelson Polsby (1968), Charles Bullock (1970), H. Douglas Price (1971), and Fiorina, Rohde and Wissel (1975) all documented various elements of the nearly interminable House careers of the period.

So, as the decade of the 1960s ended, all was right with the world of congressional careers. Members of Congress were behaving as political scientists and others expected they would. The relationship seemed clear; Congress became a nicer place and, as a result, more members stayed around to enjoy it. Voluntary retirements were scarce and careers in Congress were long. What could be simpler? But this cozy little world did not last long. In 1972 the number of voluntary retirements exploded and has never come close to returning to the low levels of the 1960s. The length of a typical career has declined steadily since 1970. And instead of aging the House is "greening" at a fairly brisk pace.

Nothing in the political science literature anticipated this turn of events, and many questions immediately arose. Why did the number of retirements go up so suddenly and so sharply? Why did the seventy-year trend in congressional careers reverse itself? What causes members of Congress to leave that presumably prestigious body?

These questions motivated the study which follows. Though I was initially attracted to the topic by the 1970s increase in retirements, I quickly became intrigued by the larger question of why members of Congress leave at all, whether in the 1970s or some other time period. By focusing on the more general issues, I feel this work takes on additional significance. Instead of being concerned only with a funny little blip in career patterns, information is provided on such fundamental issues as the motivations of our elected politicians, the role of elections in a representative democracy, and the nature of change in Congress. This is not to say no attention is given the more specific question of why there were so many retirements in the 1970s. In fact, I will have failed if this effort does not move us closer to an understanding of the processes which generated the recent increase. But a true comprehension of the causes and consequences of congressional retirement in the 1970s must be built on a foundation of general knowledge concerning the causes and consequences of the desire to leave Congress.

The plan is fairly simple. In the first three chapters I take up the question of the causes of voluntary retirement. In Chapter 1, after defining exactly what is meant by a voluntary retiree, a study is made of the variables which seem to correlate with variations in the aggregate number of retirees from twentieth-century Congresses. A completely different approach is adopted in Chapter 2. Here I report the results of twenty-four personal interviews with recently retired members of Congress. Thus, in their own words and in substantial detail retirees explain their perceptions of the reasons for their own and their colleagues' retirements. Chapter 3 also deals with retirements as individual occurrences; however, instead of relying on subjective interview data this chapter employs objective data on each representative's situation. Using these data I attempt to delineate the traits of members who retire as contrasted with those who run for re-election.

In Chapter 4 I turn my attention away from the causes of congressional retirement and toward the consequences. Does voluntary retirement matter? Is the topic worth studying? Not surprisingly, I answer the last question in the affirmative. I support this conclusion by addressing two consequences of voluntary retirement -- membership turnover and an altered relationship with constituents after the retirement decision but prior to physical departure from the House.

Chapter 5 concludes the study. In it, I tie up loose ends, summarize the findings of previous chapters, and describe some implications which flow from this analysis of voluntary retirement from the U.S. House.

CHAPTER 1

VOLUNTARY RETIREMENTS IN THE TWENTIETH-CENTURY

In my interviews with members of Congress who retired in 1978, I asked what they thought were the causes of the unusually high number of retirements from the House in the 1970s. One former representative responded with a comment that points to the requirement this chapter is designed to meet. He said:

> I don't think the number of retirements we see today is abnormally high. First we have to know what is normal. My guess is that if you collected data on the number of retirements since the Constitutional Convention, you would see that the number retiring in the 1970s is not especially out of line. It just seems unusual because of the low number of retirements in the 1950s and 1960s; and why those people stuck around so long, I don't know. You would have to ask them.

The congressman is partially correct. He is correct in his assertion that a thorough study of voluntary retirements needs to put current retirement levels in historical perspective. If this is done, we will be better able to determine if the recent increase is an unprecedented perturbation or a part of normal, perhaps cyclical fluctuations.

I have some real doubts, however, about the former congressman's suggestion that the present retirement rate is not abnormal because it is consistent with retirement rates in portions of the nineteenth-century. The House, like any institution, is undergoing constant change. Any comparison of the House in one time period with the House in another is going to violate many of the "ceteris paribus" assumptions we would like to make. Though problems of this nature are present in virtually all time-series analyses, a comparison of the nineteenth-century House with the modern House violates these assumptions in the extreme. There simply has been too much change for such comparisons, as H. Douglas Price's observations help to make clear:

> In many respects the pre-1900 House was
> similar to the average current state
> assembly: It was a part-time body (in
> session perhaps nine months out of
> twenty-four, rather than nine of
> twelve), with a high degree of member-
> ship turnover, with sharp fights for
> party leadership, and with the leaders
> in a position to make all committee
> appointments and name committee chair-
> men...Members often used bitter and
> outrageous language, scathing riducule,
> and sarcasm. Outbreaks of physical
> violence were not infrequent, and guns
> and knives were on occasion carried
> into the chamber (1971:18).

For a great deal of the time prior to 1900, as Morris
Fiorina states, "the Virginia State Legislature was
more important than the U.S. Congress" (1977:6).
Such descriptions seem a far cry from the modern
House.

There is no clear point, however, when the House
described by Price became the modern House. Fortun-
ately, there is surprising consensus that somewhere
between the mid-1890s and 1910 the House quickly
began to acquire many of the traits that have since
become its hallmarks: diminished electoral risks as
the two parties carved out regions of virtual dom-
inance, lessened overall turnover, long-run careers,
stable committees, fairly consistent application of
the seniority rule in the selection of committee
chairmen, and a total membership which stabilized at
435 (Price, 1971:14-27).

Consequently, contrary to the suggestion of the
former congressman, the period covered by this analysis will not include the nineteenth-century.[1]
Instead I intend to concentrate on variations in the
number of voluntary retirements from the House during
the twentieth-century. The major goal of this
chapter is to determine the variables which cause
these vacillations in the number of retirements.
Such a determination would provide valuable insights
into the motivations of representatives and the
nature of change in the legislative process.

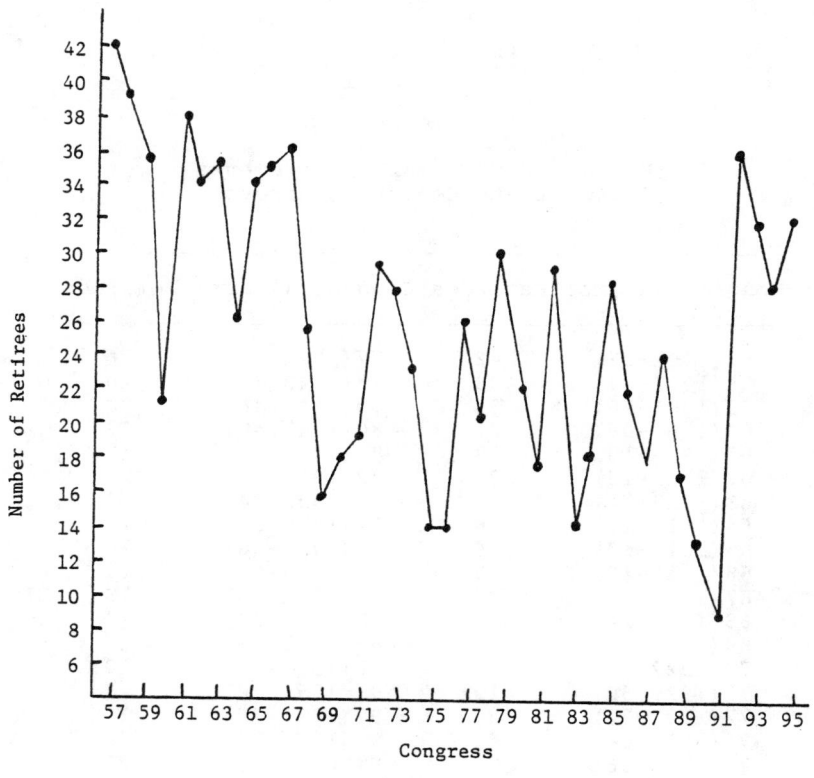

Figure 1-1. Number of Voluntary Retirements in Twentieth Century Congresses.

Table 1-1

Number of Voluntary Retirements
in Twentieth-Century Congresses

Congress(Years)	Retirees	Congress(Years)	Retirees
57(1901-02)	42	77(1941-42)	26
58(1902-04)	39	78(1943-44)	20
59(1905-06)	35	79(1945-46)	30
60(1907-08)	21	80(1947-48)	22
61(1909-10)	38	81(1949-50)	18
62(1911-12)	34	82(1951-52)	29
63(1913-14)	35	83(1953-54)	14
64(1915-16)	26	84(1955-56)	18
65(1917-18)	34	85(1957-58)	28
66(1919-20)	35	86(1959-60)	22
67(1921-22)	36	87(1961-62)	18
68(1923-24)	25	88(1963-64)	24
69(1925-26)	16	89(1965-66)	17
70(1927-28)	18	90(1967-68)	13
71(1929-30)	19	91(1969-70)	9
72(1931-32)	29	92(1971-72)	36
73(1933-34)	28	93(1973-74)	32
74(1935-36)	23	94(1975-76)	28
75(1937-38)	14	95(1977-78)	32
76(1939-40)	14	96(1979-80)	25

The Number of Voluntary Retirements

Figure 1-1 and the accompanying Table 1-1 present information on the number of representatives who voluntarily retired from each Congress in the twentieth-century. The voluntary retirement data presented in Figure 1-1 and Table 1-1 include those representatives who resigned during the pertinent Congress[2] or retired at the end of the Congress. They do <u>not</u> include those who left because of death, electoral defeat (either in primaries or general elections), appointment to another position, or a desire to attain other public office (either elective or non-elective). These exclusions are needed to keep the focus of the paper on those representatives who possessed what Schlesinger calls <u>discrete</u> ambition (1966:10). It should be noted, however, that the totals in Figure 1-1 include those who left the House to pursue private sector occupations as well as those who left in order to withdraw completely from the work force. Thus voluntary retirement is being used as a shorthand term for voluntary retirement from public service.

It is evident from Figure 1-1 that the number of voluntary retirements from the House has varied substantially over the course of the twentieth-century: from a high of 42 in the 57th Congress -- the first of this century -- to a low of 9 in the 91st Congress (1969-1970). While the line bounces around quite erratically, the overall trend is a downward one until the 1970s at which time the number of voluntary retirements shoots upwards.

In order to facilitate reading of the fairly jagged pattern in the number of voluntary retirements, I have aggregated retirements by decade. The results are presented in Figure 1-2. With the pattern smoothed out, a curvilinear pattern becomes evident. The first two decades of the century experienced very high numbers of retirements from the House (relative to the rest of the twentieth-century). In the 1920s, the number dropped to around 110 where it remained in the 1930s, 1940s, and 1950s. Then in the 1960s the number of voluntary retirements fell to 81 -- an average of only 16 per Congress. This severe drop was followed by an even more severe increase. A total of 153 representatives voluntarily retired from the Congresses of the 1970s -- a figure unmatched since the second decade of the

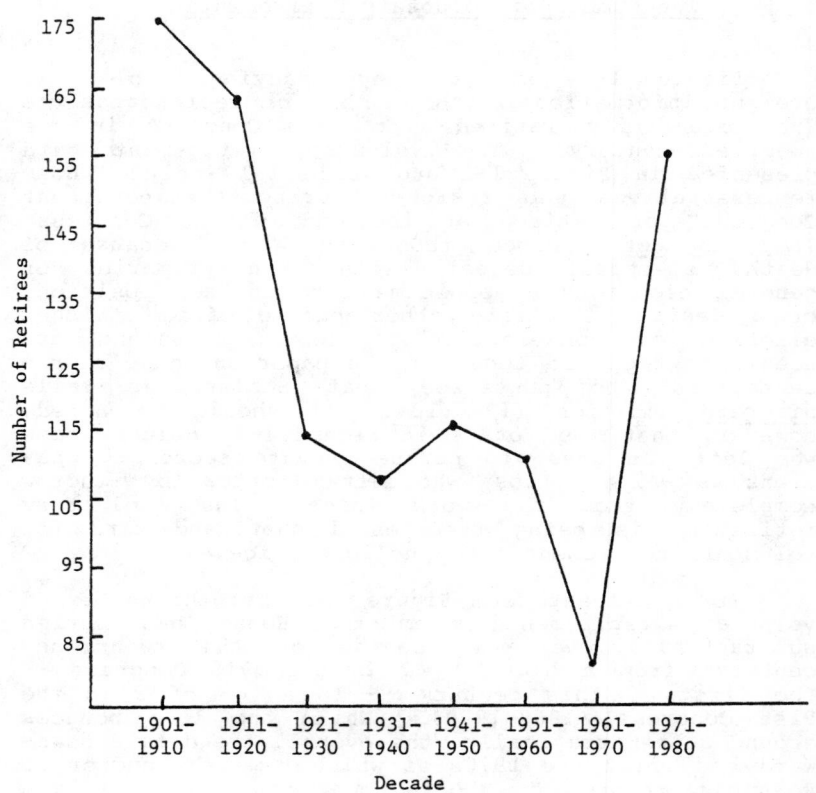

Decade	Retirees		Decade	Retirees
1901-1910	175		1941-1950	116
1911-1920	164		1951-1960	111
1921-1930	114		1961-1970	81
1931-1940	108		1971-1980	153

Figure 1-2. Number of Voluntary Retirements by Decade.

century and nearly double the number of retirees in the 1960s.

This then is the pattern I will attempt to explain in this chapter. Why has the number of retirements followed this off-center, curvilinear pattern? Why have there been so many ups and downs in the number of retirements? Why did the trend of seventy years suddenly reverse itslef in the last ten years? Several variables serve as possible answers to these questions. In the following pages I will, with varying amounts of rigor, test some of the most promising and most frequently suggested explanations.

House Retirements as Reflections of Broader Societal Changes

One possibility is that retirements from the House, like the timing and nature of retirements from any occupation, are related to larger changes in the society as a whole. There have been many changes in lifestyle and related factors in the United States over the course of the twentieth-century which could be expected to affect retirement rates. Three of these changes seem especially relevant to the topic under discussion.

Changes in Life Expectancy

It is a well-known fact that the life expectancy of someone born today is much greater than that of a person born in 1900. To be specific, the life expectancy in 1900 was only 47.3 years; by 1970 that figure had risen to nearly 71 years (Census Bureau, 1976:132). With more people living to retirement age, it could be reasonably expected that more representatives would be alive long enough to retire.

Two factors combine to cast some doubt on this hypothesis. First, there is little evidence that deaths in office occurred more frequently in the early years of the century -- something we would have expected on the basis of a "life expectancy" hypothesis. Outside of a slight increase in the 1930s, the number dying in office has remained quite stable throughout the century. Second, as mentioned previously, throughout most of the century the number of retirees was declining. How does this trend fit with the fact that the average lifespan of an American grew steadily during this same period? For the first seventy years of the century, as life expectancy grew, the number of retirees fell. In other words, the number of retirements from the House was inversely related to the average life expectancy, not positively related as the life expectancy hypothesis would lead us to predict.

Changes in Job Mobility

A second societal trend worthy of discussion is the trend toward increasing job mobility. Fred Best, in a paper prepared for the then Department of Health, Education and Welfare, describes the effects of the industrial revolution on career patterns. Best concludes:

> All in all, the available data indicates (sic) that the diversity of work -- and likely social roles -- has increased tremendously within industrializing societies; and among other things, this has vastly increased the number of options open to the individual as well as allowed a wider variance of individual talents to be utilized (1976:31-33).

Average job tenure has declined. If job is defined as working for the same employer (even if the specific position changes somewhat), job tenure has dropped from 4.8 years in 1968 to 4.5 years in 1978 (Sekscenski, 1979:48-50). Members of Congress may simply be exhibiting the characteristics of a more occupationally mobile society. This explanation is attractive in that it deals with House retirements for what most of them really are -- job changes and not retirements. From 1900 to 1970, 869 representatives voluntarily retired from the House. The Biographical Directory has information on the post-congressional activities of 747 of them. Of these 747, only 112 left the work force after their stay in Congress. Eighty-five percent of the retirees did not retire; they changed jobs. For the most part, what I am calling retirement is no such thing.

Nonetheless, the argument made above has a fairly large hole in it. Again the problem is the timing of the societal changes. According to Best and most others, the major changes in job mobility occurred very early in the twentieth-century and were the result of the industrial revolution. The job

8

flexibility made possible by the division of labor and an urbanized society has been gradually increasing in this century and, as the figures presented above show, is still increasing today. As such, this trend can hardly explain the trend in House retirements which, until the early 1970s, was toward more, not less, job stability; more, not fewer, people planning on an entire career in the House.

Changes in the Timing of Departures from the Work Force

A final societal trend I will address is the movement toward earlier retirements from all careers. The percentage of men over 65 who are in the labor force has declined fairly dramatically in the last ninety years as is evident from Figure 1-3. It may be that retiring representatives are only following a trend toward fewer working elderly -- a trend which would be anything but unique to the House.

As we have seen, however, retiring members of Congress for the most part are <u>not</u> retiring from the work force. The trend toward leaving the work force at a younger age is not relevant to 85 percent of the House retirees -- that is, those who retired from the House but did not retire from the labor force. Furthermore, the trend in the House is consistent with the overall trend for only ten out of a possible eighty years (the 1970s).

Though it is important to see the House in the context of the entire society, it is, to a great degree, a world unto itself. The job of a United States Representative is quite unlike most other occupations: it has unusual demands, unusual hours, and unusual rewards. These factors which set the job apart from most other jobs probably have a lot to do with our finding that the trend in House retirements for the most part has moved in a direction opposite that which would be predicted on the basis of overall societal trends. As individuals outside of Congress retired earlier in their lives and became more occupationally mobile, representatives became more likely to make the House a long-term career rather than a temporary position. Though this trend suddenly reversed in the 1970s and headed in a direction more consistent with the rest of society, on the whole, these overall societal trends are not helpful in explaining variations in the number of voluntary retirements from the House.

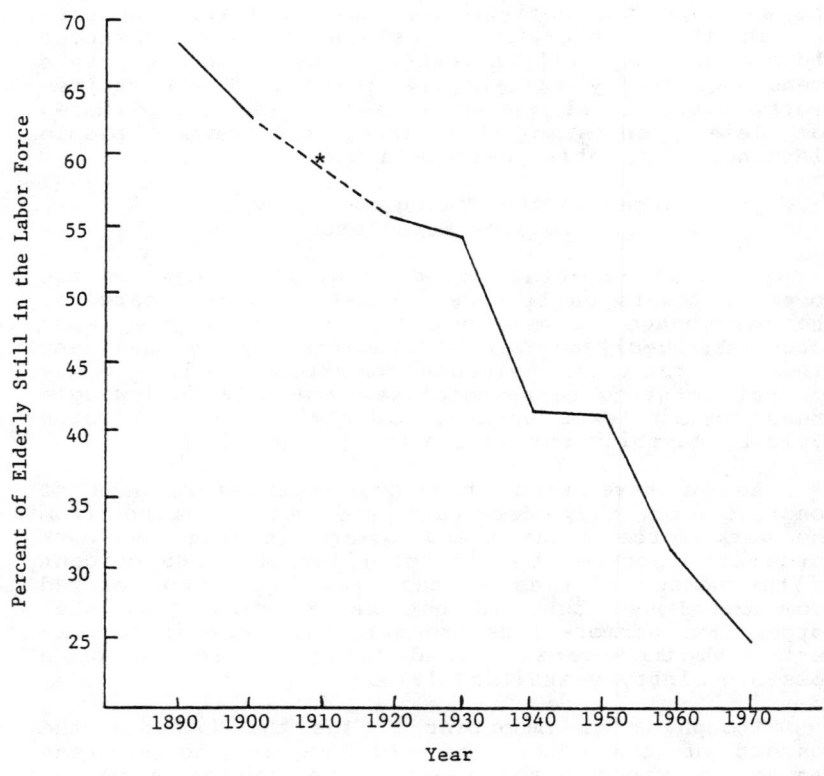

Year	Percent		Source:	Adapted from U.S.

<table>
<tr><td>Year</td><td>Percent</td><td>Source:</td><td>Adapted from U.S.
Department of Commerce,</td></tr>
<tr><td>1890</td><td>68.3</td><td></td><td>Bureau of the Census,</td></tr>
<tr><td>1900</td><td>63.1</td><td></td><td><u>Historical Statistics</u></td></tr>
<tr><td>1910</td><td>(59.3)*</td><td></td><td><u>Bicentennial Edition</u></td></tr>
<tr><td>1920</td><td>55.6</td><td></td><td>(Washington, D.C.: U.S.</td></tr>
<tr><td>1930</td><td>54.0</td><td></td><td>Government Printing</td></tr>
<tr><td>1940</td><td>41.8</td><td></td><td>Office):132.</td></tr>
<tr><td>1950</td><td>41.4</td><td></td><td></td></tr>
<tr><td>1960</td><td>30.5</td><td></td><td>*No measure taken in 1910. Figure</td></tr>
<tr><td>1970</td><td>24.8</td><td></td><td>used here was obtained by inter-
polation.</td></tr>
</table>

Figure 1-3. Percent of Men 65 and Over Who Are Still in the Work Force.

House Retirements as Responses to Reapportionment or Redistricting

Another possibility is that the number of voluntary retirements is influenced by the redrawing of congressional district lines. When lines are changed, incumbent representatives often are forced to appeal to new constituents, sometimes in areas of the state that are unfamiliar or even politically hostile. Sometimes redistricting forces two incumbents to run against one another (assuming both want to continue serving in the House). Such situations are not attractive to most members of Congress. It is not unreasonable to expect that many would voluntarily retire rather than gear up for a race in a substantially altered district or against another incumbent. Therefore, in years in which a large amount of redistricting occurred, it is reasonable to hypothesize a great deal of voluntary retiring would also occur.

For the most part, this hypothesis would predict high numbers of retirements from the first Congress of each decade -- that is, immediately prior to the implementation of the adjustments resulting from the decennial census. Thus, we would expect the number of voluntary retirements to be high in 1902, 1912, etc. This is the expected pattern with two exceptions. In 1922 there was no reapportionment and thus there was little redistricting. The 1920 census was the first to reveal a majority of the country's population resided in urban areas. This situation caused a great deal of consternation among the members of Congress, and the result was a deadlock on the issue of reapportionment. The Reapportionment Act of 1929 stipulated there would be an automatic reapportionment shortly after each census; until that time it had been only a practice -- but a practice followed religiously with the sole exception of 1922 (Galloway and Wise, 1976:22-23; Congressional Quarterly, 1966:51-52). Another break in the pattern came in the 1960s when, due to the Supreme Court's decision in _Wesberry_ v. _Sanders_ (1964) and related cases, there was a rash of redistricting. The Wesberry decision was announced on February 17, 1964. Only three states (Colorado, Connecticut and Georgia) redistricted before the 1964 election. The real landslide of redistricting came with the 1966 election. Twenty-eight states changed their districts between the 89th (65-66) and 90th (67-68) Congresses. For comparison purposes, only twenty-three states redistricted in response to the 1960 census. Twelve additional states altered their districts effective in the 1968 election. That number dropped to five for the 1970 election before skyrocketing to thirty-nine in 1972 due to the results of the 1970 census.

In light of the facts described above, the redistricting hypothesis would predict a high number of retirements in the following years: 1902, 1912, 1932, 1942, 1952, 1962, 1966, 1968 (to a lesser extent), and 1972. These years immediately precede Congresses in which many new districts were formed; therefore, we would expect additional retirements because of the disruption of numerous district lines.

In Figure 1-4 the Congresses preceding major redistrictings are circled. These are the Congresses from which we expect high numbers of retirements. If we throw out the 1920s (because there was no major redistricting) and the 1960s (because there were several), in four of the six remaining decades in this century(and nearly five of six because the 62nd Congress of 1911-12 had just one less retirement than the 63rd) the highest number of retirements came immediately prior to the major redistricting. Only the 1940s were exceptional years, and it could be argued that World War II made the early portions of that decade a special case.

Though this hypothesis exhibits some potential, there are two quite important negative factors. The first is the crucial decade of the 1960s. According to the redistricting hypothesis, this decade should have been characterized by the most retirements. Due to the Supreme Court's actions, as well as the tradi- tional redistricting in 1962, virtually every district in the country was altered in some way. Yet this is the decade with by far the fewest retirements -- only 81 -- in this century. Further, the highest number of retirements during the 1960s came before the only Congress for which not many states were redistricted (as mentioned previously, only three states made changes that were relevant to the 1964 election, yet the 88th Congress had the most retir- ees), thus constituting an exact reversal of the predictions based on the redistricting hypothesis.

The second problem with this hypothesis is that it does not explain the large trends in the number of retirements evident in Figure 1-2. Though there is

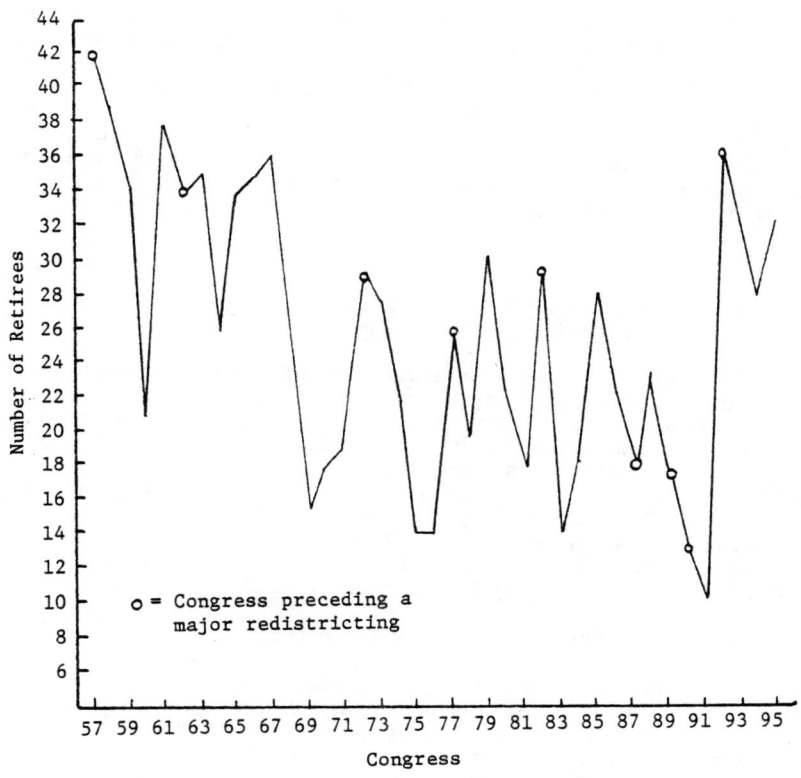

Congresses Preceding Major Redistrictings

57th
62nd
72nd
77th
82nd
87th
89th
90th (to some extent)
92nd

Figure 1-4. Congresses Preceding Major Redistrictings Matched with the Number of Voluntary Retirements.

some evidence redistricting is relevant to the number of retirements, it seems other variables must be entertained if we are to explain more than the fact that a local maximum is frequently reached immediately prior to many of the redistrictings of this century. If we are to gain a more complete understanding of the long decline and recent resurgence in the number of voluntary retirements from the House, we must look beyond the amount of redistricting which took place.

Retirements as Responses to the Monetary Incentives of the House

Yet another plausible notion is that most retirement decisions are based on monetary incentives. I will treat two hypotheses relating to monetary factors. The first holds that if the monetary rewards of being a representative are high, the number of retirements will be low. The second is that if the monetary rewards of <u>not</u> being a representative are high (because of a lucrative pension plan or attractive salaries in the private sector), the number of retirements will be high.

The Congressional Salary

Testing the first hypothesis is complicated by the fact that it is not easy to ascertain the total monetary benefits of being a representative. Even without considering the question of the acceptance of inappropriate monies or favors, many of the benefits of serving in Congress are not related to the salary received. For example, in 1945 the Joint Committee on the Organization of Congress recommended an annual salary for senators and representatives of $15,000 and the elimination of a $2,500 non-taxable expense allowance which had just been given to members of Congress (salary at the time was $10,000). In the Legislative Reorganization Act of 1946, however, Congress amended the Joint Committee's recommendation, voting to increase the salary to only $12,500 but to maintain the expense allowance. This increase took effect in 1947, but in 1951 Congress voted to eliminate the "tax-free" provision on the expense allowance. All these changes substantially altered the rewards of congressional service without changing the salary (Congressional Quarterly, 1977:31).

In addition to expense accounts and "tax-free" provisions, many other factors usually referred to as congressional "perks" combine to alter the value of a House seat. These factors include staff allowances (for trips to the district as well as for trips of official business outside the district), allowances for stationery, newsletters, office equipment, and publications, life and health insurance, access to health care, tax breaks (because most representatives are virtually forced to maintain two households -- one in Washington and one in the district), and even such things as access to T.V. recording facilities in the Rayburn House Office Building, a free health club, and special prices for barber and beauty shop services (Congressional Quarterly, 1977:33-49).

The purpose here is not to make a case for or against the necessity of these perquisites of office, but to point out the problems these many forms of compensation raise for ascertaining the total remuneration of a member of Congress. Perquisites have been added at various times in the history of Congress, usually with as little ceremony as possible. Their usage has been monitored with varying degrees of care. For example, restrictions on so-called "slush funds" (also called office accounts) were tightened substantially in 1978. One anonymous congressman called these slush funds "...the last refuge for members of Congress who want to take unlimited amounts of money from any source, spend it on whatever they please and report it nowhere" (Walters, 1975). Therefore, tightening the restrictions on the use of these slush funds profoundly affected the monetary rewards of some congressmen. Likewise, limitations on outside income earned via honoraria and the like affect the value of a seat in the House.

These complications, combined with the fact that the expected outlays of members of Congress have changed appreciably, make it virtually impossible to compute objectively the dollar value of a seat in the House, although such computations have been attempted.[3] With strict quantification of all congressional rewards and obligations nearly impossible, my analysis will concentrate on only one aspect of the package -- the congressional salary. Figure 1-5 shows the salary level for members of Congress as well as the number of retirees.

Though at first glance the two trends may not look much alike, there seems to be some connection in the first fifty years of the century. Salary jumped 50 percent in the 60th Congress, and the number of retirements was off sharply. The number of retirements then rose and stayed high as the salary was not increased for nearly twenty years. The next increase (in 1925) also brought a sharp drop in the number of retirements as most members wanted to take advantage of the improved salary. The number of retirees then went up in the early 1930s as the salary level stayed the same and even dropped slightly. Declines in the number of retirees were registered in the 74th and 80th Congresses; both of these witnessed salary increases. Only in the more recent years does the relationship seem to weaken (although even then the fairly massive salary increases of 1965 and 1969 were met with extremely small numbers of retirees).

Part of the reason for the apparent weakening of the relationship may be the factor alluded to previously -- the complications caused by the proliferation and adjustment of congressional perquisites. Before the 1950s and 1960s, the legislative salary was a good measure of the benefits of being a representative; expense accounts, large staff allowances, recording studios, and the like were not a part of a representative's life. In the last twenty years these factors have become vital, and there have been fairly wild oscillations in the opportunities of representatives to use and misuse these benefits. Thus, one possible explanation for the findings presented in Figure 1-5 is that there was a time when salary was an acceptable measure of benefits received, but in the 1960s and 1970s it no longer was. The breakdown may be not in the relationship of benefits received to the number of retirements but in the measure of benefits received.

A second possibility is that representatives respond more to variations in the real worth rather than the level of the congressional salary. To test this notion, I have computed the worth of congressional salaries by adjusting them by the appropriate consumer price index (CPI). For example, because the CPI was .25 in 1901 and 1902, the $5,000 congressional salary for the 57th Congress adjusts to $20,000 in 1967 dollars. The results of these computations are displayed in Figure 1-6 and Table 1-2.

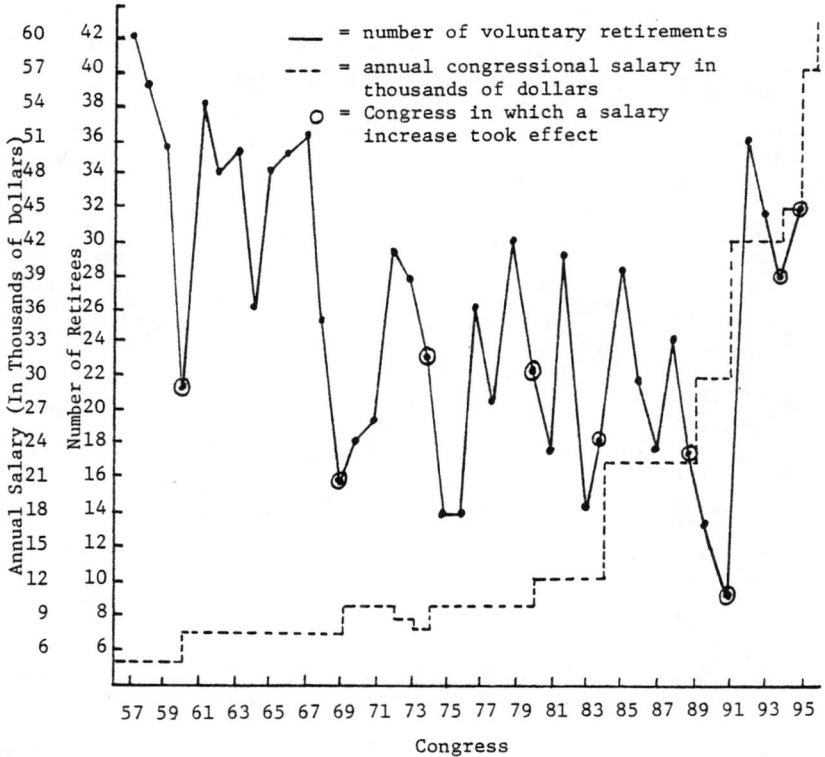

Years	Congressional Salary	Years	Congressional Salary
1900-1907	$5,000	1947-1955	$12,500
1907-1925	$7,500	1955-1965	$22,500
1925-1932	$10,000	1965-1969	$30,000
1932-1933	$9,000	1969-1975	$42,500
1933-1935	$8,500	1975-1977	$44,600
1935-1947	$10,000	1977-1979	$57,500
		1979-	$61,660

Source: Portions adapted from Congressional Quarterly, Congressional Ethics (Washington, D.C.: Congressional Quarterly, Inc., 1977):30.

Figure 1-5. Congressional Salary and the Number of Voluntary Retirements.

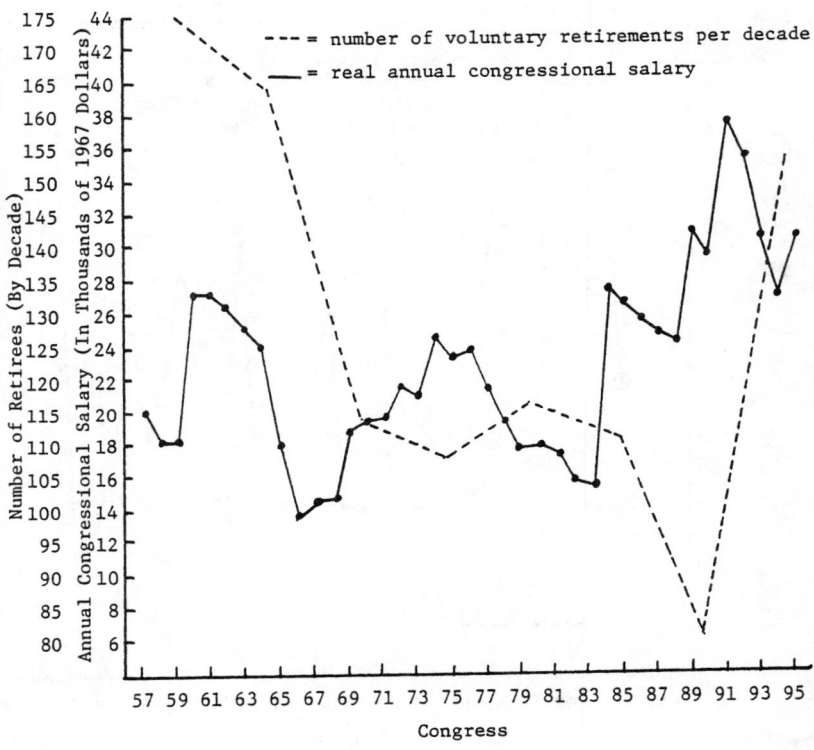

Figure 1-6. Real Annual Congressional Salary and the Number of Voluntary Retirements.

Table 1-2

Real (1967 Dollars) Annual Congressional Salary in Twentieth-Century Congresses

Congress	Salary	Congress	Salary
57	$20,000	77	$21,551
58	$18,518	78	$19,120
59	$18,518	79	$17,793
60	$27,272	80	$17,959
61	$27,272	81	$17,421
62	$26,315	82	$15,893
63	$25,083	83	$15,556
64	$23,809	84	$27,846
65	$17,964	85	$26,331
66	$13,416	86	$25,568
67	$14,450	87	$24,972
68	$14,662	88	$24,377
69	$18,957	89	$31,282
70	$19,361	90	$29,382
71	$19,743	91	$37,610
72	$21,966	92	$34,468
73	$21,546	93	$30,270
74	$24,213	94	$26,883
75	$23,529	95	$30,585
76	$23,923		

The pattern of real income for members of Congress is revealing in itself. Until the 1960s, congressional salaries bounced around in the range of $20,000 to $27,000 except for two noticeable dips -- one down as low as $14,000 per year (in 1967 dollars). In the 1960s, real salary rose fairly sharply, topping off at nearly $38,000 in the 91st Congress before dropping somewhat in the 1970s.

But our primary concern is with the relationship of changes in real salary and the number of voluntary retirements from the House. The expected relationship is _negative_ since a high salary should cause the number of retirements to be low while a low real salary should make it easier for many members to retire voluntarily. Although the 91st Congress of 1969-70 had both the highest real income and smallest number of retirees, we see that in the main the predicted inverse relationship does not materialize. This relationship will be analyzed more quantitatively in the last section of this chapter, but it seems as though changes in real salary do not exert a major influence on changes in the number of voluntary departures.

The Congressional Pension

An additional factor which must be considered in any treatment of monetary incentives is the existence and relative attractiveness of the congressional pension. As one congressman who retired in 1978 stated in discussing decisions to retire voluntarily, "A man lies if he says the pension is not a factor" (Bethel, 1979).

Retired members of Congress did not always have a pension plan to encourage their retirement decisions. Before the Legislative Reorganization Act of 1946, former members of Congress, whether retired voluntarily or involuntarily, received no pension benefits at all. This act, however, placed members of Congress under the Civil Service Retirement Act. Contributions of 6 percent of salary brought annuities of 2 1/2 percent of some computation of a member's average salary times the number of years of service (with an annuity maximum of 80 percent of the member's final salary). With minor modifications (in 1954, for example, the minimum age for receiving benefits was reduced from 62 to 60), the basic plan remained unchanged until the late 1960s when it was made substantially more attractive. In 1967 a "cost-of-living" escalator was added to pension benefits, and in 1969 the base for annuity computations was changed from the mean of the <u>five</u> highest salaried years to the mean of the <u>three</u> highest salaried years. Also, in 1969, a "kicker" payment was added to make up for the delay between the time the cost of living went up and the time it rose enough to trigger a raise in annuities. (In 1976 this "kicker" was replaced by an automatic six-month adjustment based on changes in the consumer price index.) The maximum pension still is 80 percent of the highest annual salary, but the minimum age for receiving partial benefits has been reduced to 55.

If retirements are influenced by the attractiveness of the pension plan, the number of retirees should be low whenever there is a pay raise because members will want to stick around long enough to allow the higher salary to become a part of their annuity base. Then one or two Congresses after the pay raise there should be an increase in the number of voluntary retirements. For example, some have claimed that the large number of retirees in 1972 was produced by the fact that since the base period was lowered to three years, the annuities for those retiring in 1972 would be based entirely on a salary of $42,500 (in 1969 the salary was increased from $30,000 to $42,500) (Bethel, 1979).

This logic leads us to predict large groups of retirees from the 80th and 81st Congresses (the first groups eligible for pensions), the 85th and 86th (due to pay increase in the 84th), the 90th (after the pay increase of the 89th), and the 92nd and 93rd (due to the substantial pay increase of the 91st as well as the shortening of the base period). Figure 1-7 shows the pattern in the number of retirements with circles around the years we would expect large groups of retirees given the pension plan hypothesis.

Of the seven predictions based on the pension plan hypothesis, only two or perhaps three are accurate (large groups of retirees in the 92nd and 93rd and a fairly large group in the 85th). On the whole, retirement rates prior to the institution of the pension plan actually were higher than they were after 1946 when the pension plan began. Though the pension plan may be a contributing factor in many decisions to retire from the House, this factor cannot adequately explain variations in the number of retirees over the course of the twentieth-century.

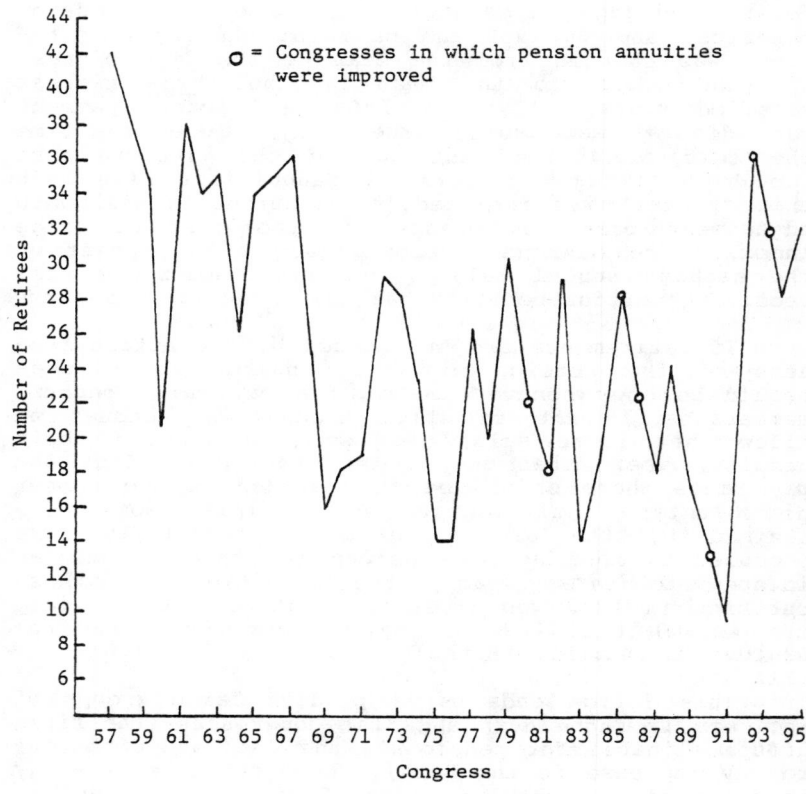

Figure 1-7.   Improvements in the Pension Annuities and
the Number of Voluntary Retirements.

Retirements as Responses to Varying
Levels of Party Competition

A further plausible hypothesis is that retirement decisions are responses to electoral pressures -- that some retire in order to avoid the ignominy of electoral defeat. If this were true, we would expect more retirements in times when there is intense party competition and fewer retirements in times when many districts are dominated by one party election after election. H. Douglas Price puts great emphasis on the realignment of 1896 -- a realignment which left most of the country safely in the hands of one party or the other -- as a factor in making the House a more prestigous, more professional, more secure, and in general a more pleasureable place to be. It is not inconsistent with such thinking to speculate that variations in the level of party competition may affect the number of people who want to leave the House, either because of a fear of electoral defeat or a more general feeling that the body is not a nice place to be.

There are many measures of electoral competition which could be employed. The measure used here is one employed by Charles O. Jones (1964:435). It is the number of times in a given election that a member of one party succeeded a member of the other party in obtaining a seat in the House. Jones presents this information from 1914 to 1960, aggregated by decade. I have computed the figures for the two decades since 1960. I have also adjusted Jones' computations for the first time period which, instead of five elections, is actually seven elections.

As Figure 1-8 shows, throughout most of this century both the level of party competition (as measured by the number of changes in the party that represents individual districts) and the number of voluntary retirements have declined. This much is consistent with what we would predict on the basis of the party competition hypothesis: the level of competition goes down, more people feel safe, the House becomes more stable and more pleasant, and as a result the number of voluntary departures also goes down.

But the hypothesis fails a major test: the degree of party competition is _not_ able to predict the dramatic surge in voluntary retirements which occurred in the 1970s. Though the level of competi-

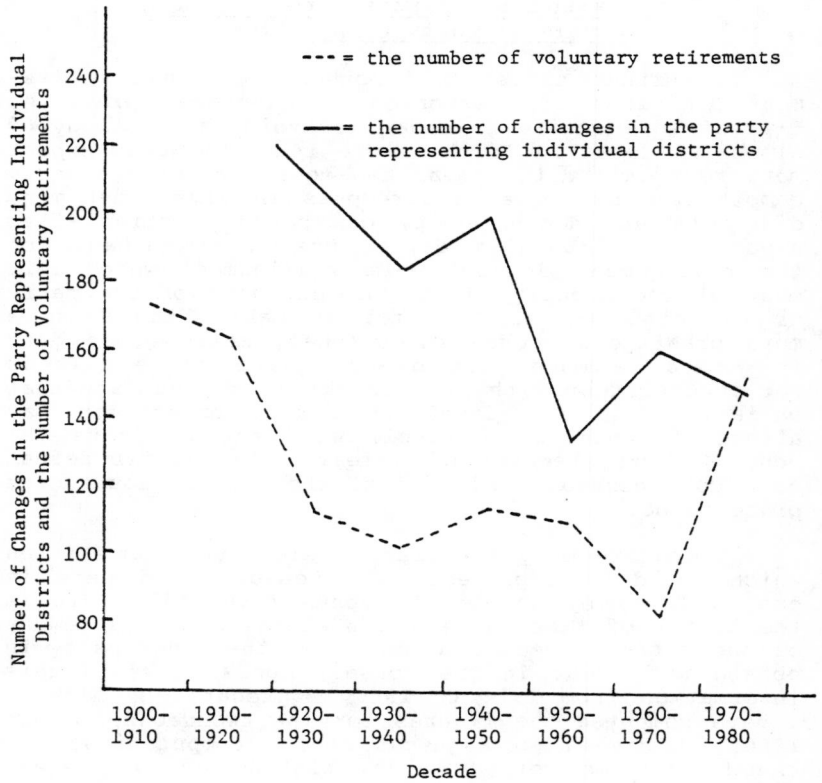

Figure caption and legend:

--- = the number of voluntary retirements

— = the number of changes in the party representing individual districts

Y-axis: Number of Changes in the Party Representing Individual Districts and the Number of Voluntary Retirements

X-axis: Decade

| 1900–1910 | 1910–1920 | 1920–1930 | 1930–1940 | 1940–1950 | 1950–1960 | 1960–1970 | 1970–1980 |

Years	Number of Party Switches	Source:
1914–1926	308 (220)*	Portions adapted from Charles Jones,
1932–1940	184	Inter-Party
1942–1950	199	Competition for
1952–1960	135	Congressional
1962–1970	160	Seats," Western
1972–1980	149	Political Quarterly 17 (Sept. 1964):465.

*308 for this irregular time period converts to 220 for a standard five-Congress time period.

Figure 1-8. The Number of District Party Switches and the Number of Voluntary Retirements.

tion for House seats has declined in the last 15 years (see the literature on the vanishing marginals, especially Mayhew, 1974a), the number of retirements has gone up dramatically. Contrary to expectations, greater safety has not led more representatives to seek re-election. While accurate in selected time periods, the level of competition hypothesis fails as an overall predictor of changes in the number of voluntary retirements.

Retirements as Responses to the Health of the Seniority Rule

Yet another possible explanation for variations in the number of retirements is the fluctuating usage of the seniority rule as a means, among other things, of selecting committee chairmen. According to Richard Fenno, one of the three things members of Congress want to do is to maximize their power within the body (1973:1). In Congress this means maximize committee power. We might reasonably expect, therefore, that if members know they have a committee chair waiting for them at the end of their career, they would be more likely to try to hang on until they have that post. They will be less likely to retire since they have capital stored up in the form of their accumulated years of service. Furthermore, those who have the chairmanships will not be anxious to give up these "plum" positions since they had to wait so long to obtain them. Knowing that the chairs are theirs as long as they are returned to office makes life in the House much more comfortable for these individuals.

For many years knowledge about committee leadership positions was simplified and security was enhanced by the seniority rule -- an unwritten congressional norm holding that the majority party member with the longest consecutive service on a committee will be its chairman. This seniority rule has been applied in various degrees over the course of the twentieth-century. Nelson Polsby, et al., have collected data on the percent of the time the seniority rule was followed in the selection of committee chairmen (1969). I have calculated this indicator through the 96th Congress, and in Figure 1-9 and Table 1-3, this information is presented along with the trend in the number of voluntary retirements.

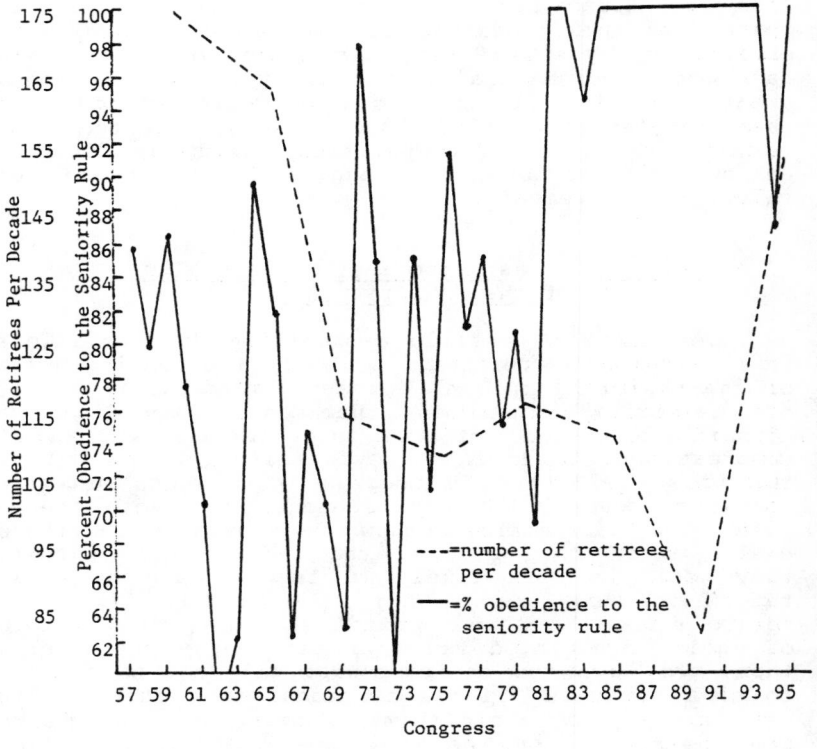

Source: Portions adapted from Nelson Polsby, et al.,
          "The Growth of the Seniority System in the
          U.S. House of Representatives," _American
          Political Science Review_ 63 (September 1969):
          793.

Figure 1-9.   Obedience to the Seniority Rule (in the
              Selection of Committee Chairmen) and the
              Number of Voluntary Retirements.

Table 1-3

Obedience to the Seniority Rule in the Selection of
Committee Chairmen in Twentieth-Century Congresses

Congress	% Obey	Congress	% Obey
57	85.9	77	84.7
58	79.6	78	75.5
59	86.4	79	80.4
60	77.6	80	69.2
61	70.0	81	100.0
62	48.0	82	100.0
63	62.2	83	94.4
64	89.2	84	100.0
65	81.8	85	100.0
66	61.4	86	100.0
67	74.6	87	100.0
68	70.2	88	100.0
69	62.7	89	100.0
70	97.7	90	100.0
71	84.4	91	100.0
72	60.0	92	100.0
73	84.4	93	100.0
74	71.1	94	86.5
75	91.3	95	100.0
76	80.4		

Figure 1-9 shows that the trend in the application of the seniority rule is one which exhibited some sign of reversal in the 1970s. As such, it matches the voluntary retirement trend better than most of the variables we have been trying, since, as we already know, the voluntary retirement trend also reversed in the 1970s. But has the trend in the application of the seniority rule really reversed? Does the fact that in 1975 three congressmen were "entitled to" but denied committee chairs really constitute a reversal in the vitality of the seniority rule?

Some have argued that the events of 1975 were highly unusual, idiosyncratic and, as such, unlikely to be repeated (Hinckley, 1976:398). The fact that there were no "coups" in the 95th or 96th Congresses lends support to this view. But regardless of whether or not the events of 1975 are repeated, the important fact is that, in Barbara Hinckley's words, "Precedents now have been shattered" (1976:398). The important change for our purposes is not that three committee chairmen were deposed, but that those who hold or, according to the cannons of the seniority rule, are close to obtaining committee chairs can never feel secure about their positions. The revival of the Democratic caucus may not have manifested itself in the depositions of numerous "senior" chairmen every two years but, as Congressman Thomas S. Foley (D.-Wash.) states, it is now known there is "a kind of gun behind the door" (Congressional Quarterly, 1979:35). As a result, the changes go far beyond the picture portrayed in Figure 1-9, which presented only a slight dip in the 95th Congress surrounded by perfect, 100 percent obedience scores. The extent of the change is more easily understood if we analyze the events relating to the seniority rule in the 1970s a little more closely.

The changes actually began in early 1969. At this time the caucus of the Democratic majority was given more bite as a result of two provisions: one calling for monthly meetings, the other facilitating open discussion in the meetings. In the next few years, these provisions served as a basis for chipping away at the position of entrenched committee chairmen -- the most important early change being a provision that chairmen would be elected by secret ballot in the caucus. Then in 1970 the caucus created the Committee on Study, Organization and Review, headed by Julia Butler Hansen (D.-Wash.), which was given the task of studying the seniority system. When they were organizing for the 92nd Congress in January of 1971, the Democrats announced that the Democratic Committee on Committees (then the members of the Ways and Means Committee) need not consider seniority in formulating its recommendation on chairmanships. More important, any ten Democrats were given the right to obtain a separate vote on any individual chairman (thereby making it easier to attack one chairman without voting against the whole slate of "senior" chairs). These alterations came after the committee chairmen had been weakened by changes which strengthened the autonomy of subcommittees. Thus, even in the 92nd Congress (1971-72), the writing was on the wall for committee chairmen. The caucus had given itself the power and it had even started to use it. In 1971, Representative John McMillan (D.-S.C.), chairman of the District of Columbia Committee, was subjected to an individual vote in accordance with the wishes of at least ten members of the caucus. McMillan won the vote (126 to 96) and retained the chairmanship, but many members were beginning to feel the presence of the "gun behind the door" (Galloway and Wise, 1976:75).

Although further changes were made by the Democrats when they were organizing for the 93rd Congress in 1973 -- the most important made a secret ballot easier to demand -- all senior members on the committees were elected to their respective chairmanships. Nonetheless, as Sidney Wise writes in his revision of George Galloway's History of the House of Representatives:

> the fact that a considerable number of negative ballots were cast against Representatives W.R. Poage of Texas, Wayne L. Hays of Ohio, Chet Holifield of California, and Wright Patman of Texas, and that the voting results became public, put each chairman on notice that his style was not beyond criticism (1976:76).

The stage was set for the dramatic events of 1975. Not only were three senior chairmen -- Patman, Poage, and F. Edward Hebert -- unceremoniously dumped, but Wilbur Mills of Arkansas was motivated to abort efforts to retain his prestigious Ways and Means chair because of unrest in the caucus and elsewhere over his much-publcized antics. Still another powerful chairman, Wayne Hays, beat back a concerted effort to deny him the top position on the House Administrative Committee. Even more violations of the seniority rule may have occurred except that five incumbent chairmen (not counting Mills) did not attempt to be re-elected (four voluntarily retired and one switched committees) (Congressional Quarterly, 1979:44). In addition to all these changes in committee chairs, two important subcommittee heads -- Leonor Sullivan (D.-Mo.) and Harley Staggers (D.-W.V.) -- also lost their chairmanships.

Many people view the organization of the 95th Congress in 1977 as a return to the "old ways," but while no senior chairmen were toppled, many negative votes were again cast, especially against Robert Nix (D.-Pa.) of the Post Office and Civil Service Committee. Again, a sizable block of senior members decided not to take their chances in the caucus: eight of the twenty-two standing committees in the House were headed by new chairmen in 1977 (Congressional Quarterly, 1979:45). And there was still a major ouster in 1977. Robert L.F. Sikes (D.-Fl.), the representative with the longest service in the House of any congressman in Florida's history, was defeated for the chairmanship of the House Military Construction Appropriations Subcommittee by a resounding vote of 189-93, even though according to the seniority rule it should have continued to be his. Things were anything but back to normal.

No senior committee chairmen were thrown out with the beginning of the 96th Congress in 1979, but Congressional Quarterly observed that "the time-honored seniority system took a beating in the House Jan. 30 and 31, 1979, as three junior Democrats bumped more senior colleagues in electioins for subcommittee chairmanships on the Commerce and Government Operations committees" (1979:64).

The point is that though there have been only three clear violations of the seniority rule at the full committee level in the 1970s, these cases together with a number of close calls, several defeats of senior members at the subcommittee level, and a general weakening of the power of committee chairs combine to produce an atmosphere which is not conducive to senior chairmen wanting to hold on as long as possible. To those who had known what it was to be unquestioned committee bosses, such changes must have been both disorienting and disappointing.

But changes in the seniority rule have affected not only committee chairmen; younger members no longer are as likely to plan a long-term career, aspiring to committee chairmanship as the reward for long service. Since seniority no longer is the sine qua non in the selection of committee chairmen, members think little of retiring after ten or twelve years. If the seniority rule were universally applied, it would be very difficult to throw away twelve years of "dues paying" by deciding to retire.

The magnitude of the 1970s changes in seniority is not picked up by the measure employed in Figure 1-9. Indeed, H. Douglas Price may be correct when he states "a strict seniority system is a dichotomous variable. It is either present or absent" (1977:41). A strict seniority system would be present if the members were absolutely sure the seniority rule was going to be followed.

If, following Price's suggestion, we attempt to dichotomize seniority, we would have something that corresponds quite closely with the curvilinear retirement pattern. As Polsby points out, violations of seniority around the turn of the century were fairly frequent and in general were uncompensated violations. This means "potential chairmen whose seniority was violated" were not compensated with..."chairmanships of other committees or party leadership positions" (1969:794). This situation quickly changed and, according to Price, "strict seniority, which had meant almost nothing in the House as of 1900, had come to mean almost everything in naming committee chairmen and ranking members by 1920" (1975:16). From the 1920s until the very early 1970s, there were very few violations of the seniority rule, and when there were, the victims usually were placated with a consolation price such as another committee chairmanship or a party leadership position -- actions representative of an attitude of conciliation definitely not present in the Democratic caucus of the 1970s.

Thus, change in the seniority system cannot be ruled out as a cause of variations in the number of retirees. When the seniority rule has not been followed strictly -- in the early years of this century and in the 1970s -- the retirement rate has been quite high. When the seniority rule has been virtual law in the selection of committee chairmen, the resultant premium placed on long tenure seems to have reduced the number of members who wanted to put a voluntary end to their House careers.

Retirements as Responses to the Institution-
alization of the House

Since it was first circulated in 1964, Price's article, "The Congressional Career: Then and Now" (Polsby, 1971), has made many scholars aware of the benefits of looking at Congress in an historical framework. Studies by Witmer, Polsby, Bullock, and Fiorina, Rohde and Wissel, all written in the late 1960s or early 1970s, adopted such an approach and all came to quite similiar conclusions: the House in the 1950s and 1960s had become a place for a career. No longer were people fleeing Washington "almost as fast as was humanly possible" (Price, 1975:5). Polsby put this trend into perspective by calling it part of the "institutionalization" of the House. This institutionalization involved many things, and Polsby's classic article explores several of them: the development of boundaries which set it apart from the environment, increasing complexity (division of labor, regularized movement from role to role, etc.), and the employment of universalistic rather than particularistic criteria for conducting business (development of precedents, rules, traditions and the like). On the whole, according to Bullock, "the institutionalization of the House has made it a more predictable and professional place." Not surprisingly, many would speculate along with Bullock that this institutionalization would be "an additional reason for members not to retire" (1972:1295).

For most of the twentieth-century, this expectation has proved accurate. All the historical works mentioned above note a trend toward longer careers and less turnover. Polsby provides evidence that the mean number of terms of service is up and the percent of first-term members is down (1968). This theme is echoed by Bullock. He notes that the number of representatives who have served ten terms or more increased from 11 in the 62nd Congress (1911-1912) to 87 in the 92nd (1971-1972) (Bullock, 1972). Witmer finds that the ratio of first-termers to ten-termers was 27 to 1 when Theodore Roosevelt took office, but only '.6 to 1 by the time John F. Kennedy was president vitmer, 1964). Price presents similar evidence in graphic form (1971:17) and the change is indeed quite drastic. Fiorina, Rohde and Wissel note that turnover, despite fluctuation here and there, has for the most part declined during the twentieth-century (1975:33). The institutionalization of the House was having the expected effect.

But just as all the pieces fell into place in the early 1970s, changes began to occur. The average age of representatives went down, average tenure went down,[4] the number of ten-termers dropped quite sharply (Dodd and Oppenheimer, 1977:23), no longer was an apprenticeship period necessary before acquiring a position of influence, decisions at times were more particularistic and less determined by universalistic criteria such as the seniority rule, and (the most important change for our purposes) the number of voluntary retirements increased significantly. The predictable, professional, institutionalized House had become increasingly less predictable and, if not less professional, certainly less experienced.

This is not the place for a comprehensive analysis of the changes taking place in the House. The point here is that expectations based on the institutionalization of the House, though consistent with the declining number of retirees from 1900 to 1970, do not explain the sharp upturn in the number of retirees during the 1970s. In fact, these notions, because they have become such an accepted part of the folklore of congressional research, make the increased number of retirees even more baffling. Why, if the House is a better place to be, are there so many who do not want to be there? While talk of a de-institutionalization seems premature, the spate of high-quality articles around the late-1960s which documented various facets of the House's institutionalization seems to have made us slow to acknowledge the startling changes in the makeup of the body which have taken place in the 1970s.

A precise operationalization of the concept of institutionalization is not easy; however, a simple counter variable may not do too much disservice to the notion. The consensus seems to be that the march toward institutionalization has been a slow and steady one throughout the twentieth-century. Evidence presented by Polsby and others indicates no sudden surges, or reversals, but a consistent and moderate movement -- a movement classified as "monotonic" by William Mishler, et al. (1973:363).

Therefore, I have represented the concept of institutionalization with a counter variable which starts at 0 for the 57th Congress (1901-02) and ends at 38 for the 95th Congress (1977-78). Such a variable seems to match fairly well with the number of voluntary retirements through the 1960s, but as mentioned above, institutionalization certainly is not able to explain the 1970s increase in retirements from the House.

A Formal Test of the Potential Causes of Voluntary Retirements

Until now I have relied upon past literature, common sense, and "eyeballing" graphs to get some notion of the events which might be able to explain variations in the number of voluntary retirements. In the last section of this chapter, I turn to a more systematic test of the hypotheses.

This test will utilize eight variables (some other variables discussed in this chapter, like the broader societal changes, and the level of party competition, are not included because it was obvious they did not fit with the retirement trend) and thirty-nine cases (the thirty-nine Congresses of the twentieth-century). The complete data set is presented in Table 1-4.

The first variable is the dependent variable -- the number of voluntary resignations and retirements from each Congress (for reasons other than a desire to run for a new public office). Thus, the numbers in the second column of Table 1-4 are the same as those plotted in Figure 1-1. The first independent variable is dichotomous and represents the presence or absence of a major redistricting subsequent to the Congress. One (1) is coded in those Congresses which are circled in Figure 1-4, and zero (0) is coded for all other Congresses. The second independent variable, also dichotomous, represents the presence or absence of a salary increase in the relevant Congress. The third independent variable is the average of the real value of the congressional salary for the two years of each Congress. As such, the figures in the fifth column of Table 1-4 correspond with those plotted in Figure 1-6. The fourth independent variable is another dichotomous variable. This one represents improvements in the pension plan in accordance with our earlier discussion of the topic

34

Table 1-4

The Number of Retirements and the Values of Selected Independent Variables for Twentieth-Century Congresses

Congress	Number of Retirements	Redistricting	Salary Increase	Real Salary	Pension Improvements	% Obey Seniority Rule	Dichotomized Seniority	Institutionalization
57	42	1	0	20.0	0	86	0	0
58	39	0	0	18.5	0	80	0	1
59	35	0	0	18.5	0	86	0	2
60	21	0	1	27.3	0	78	0	3
61	38	0	0	27.3	0	70	0	4
62	34	1	0	26.3	0	48	0	5
63	35	0	0	25.1	0	62	0	6
64	26	0	0	23.8	0	89	0	7
65	34	0	0	18.0	0	82	0	8
66	35	0	0	13.4	0	61	0	9
67	36	0	0	14.4	0	75	1	10
68	25	0	0	14.7	0	70	1	11
69	16	0	1	19.0	0	63	1	12
70	18	0	0	19.4	0	98	1	13
71	19	0	0	19.7	0	84	1	14
72	29	1	0	22.0	0	60	1	15
73	28	0	0	21.5	0	84	1	16
74	23	0	1	24.2	0	71	1	17
75	14	0	0	23.6	0	91	1	18

Table 1-4
(Continued)

Congress	Number of Retirements	Redistricting	Salary Increase	Real Salary	Pension Improvements	% Obey Seniority Rule	Dichotomized Seniority	Institutionalization
76	14	0	0	23.9	0	80	1	19
77	26	1	0	21.6	0	85	1	20
78	30	0	0	19.1	0	75	1	21
79	30	0	0	17.8	0	80	1	22
80	22	0	1	18.0	1	69	1	23
81	18	0	0	17.4	1	100	1	24
82	29	1	0	15.9	0	100	1	25
83	14	0	0	15.6	0	94	1	26
84	18	0	1	27.8	0	100	1	27
85	28	0	0	26.3	1	100	1	28
86	22	0	0	25.6	1	100	1	29
87	18	0	0	25.0	0	100	1	30
88	24	0	0	24.4	0	100	1	31
89	17	1	1	31.3	0	100	1	32
90	13	1	0	29.4	0	100	1	33
91	9	0	1	37.6	0	100	1	34
92	36	1	0	34.5	1	100	0	35
93	32	0	0	30.3	1	100	0	36
94	28	0	1	26.9	1	86	0	37
95	32	0	1	30.6	1	100	0	38

(see Figure 1-7). The fifth independent variable is the percentage of the cases in which the seniority rule was followed in the selection of committee chairmen (see Figure 1-9). The sixth independent variable is a dichotomous variable registering the presence or absence of a strict seniority system. The final variable is a counter variable which represents the gradual institutionalization of the House.

More detailed explanations of the variables and the measurement techniques are contained in the earlier pages of this chapter. Table 1-5 summarizes our expectations based on these hypotheses, given the way the variables are measured. Table 1-5 also contains the actual correlations of the independent variables with the dependent variable.

The correlations are quite close to our expectations. As measured here, improvements in the pension plan are <u>not</u> positively related to the number of voluntarily retiring representatives (something we would expect if retirement decisions were generally based upon a desire to take advantage of improved pension benefits). However, this variable is not given a fair chance in that for nearly two-thirds of the time period under study (from 1900 to 1946) the pension plan was completely irrelevant to retirement decisions because it did not exist. This fact, no doubt, accounts for the extremely small coefficient for this variable, and for the fact that the sign of the coefficient is in the wrong direction.

The other variables meet our expectations quite closely. Redistricting does seem to be related to retirements (if a massive redistricting is imminent, there are large numbers of retirees), but as we suspected this relationship is not very strong. High real salaries seem to be related to low retirement levels, but there is an even stronger inverse correlation between salary increases and the number of voluntary retirements. Obedience to the seniority rule does seem to be associated with low levels of retirements, especially when measured by a dichotomous variable. Finally, the institutionalization of the House has in general been associated with fewer retirements (the correlation here would go up considerably if the last four data points were removed).

Though correlation coefficients are somewhat helpful in determining which variables covary, regression analysis comes closer to flushing out the causes

Table 1-5

Expected and Actual Correlations

Variable	Expected Correlation with the Number of Retirements	Actual Correlation with the Number of Retirements
Redistricting	Weak +	.08
Salary Increase	−	−.34
Real Salary	−	−.20
Pension Improvements	Weak +	−.01
% Obey Seniority Rule	−	−.36
Dichotomized Seniority	Strong −	−.68
Institutionalization	−	−.43

Table 1-6

Regression of the Number of Voluntary Retirements on Seven Independent Variables

Variable	Coefficient	T-Ratio		
Redistricting	2.50	1.09		
Salary Increase	-4.51*	-1.79	Constant =	51.03
Real Salary	- .39*	-1.71	R^2 =	.64
Pension Improvements	1.22	.40	D.W. =	2.05
% Obey Seniority Rule	- .11	-1.30	F =	8.03
Dichotomized Seniority	-12.28*	-4.91	N =	39
Institutionalization	.07	.44		

* = significant (.05)

Where:

Redistricting	= 1 if there was a major redistricting after the Congress: 0 if not
Salary Increase	= 1 if there was a salary increase in the Congress; 0 if not
Real Salary	= the value in 1967 dollars of the congressional salary
Pension Improvements	= 1 if the pension plan improved in some significant way; 0 if not
% Obey Seniority Rule	= The % of time the seniority rule was followed in the selection of committee chairmen
Dichotomized Seniority	= 1 if the seniority rule was virtual law; 0 if it was not
Institutionalization	= a counter from 0 to 38 representing the gradual institutionalization of the House

of variations in the number of retirements. Therefore, all the independent variables described above were regressed on the number of retirees in each Congress. The results are presented in Table 1-6.

Several elements of Table 1-6 are worth noting. The R^2 is a respectable .64, meaning that nearly two-thirds of the variance in the number of retirements is accounted for by the seven independent variables in the model.[5] The regression is unusual for a time-series in that there is virtually no autocorrelation. (The more the Durbin-Watson statistic departs from 2.00, the greater the degree of autocorrelation.) Thus, no correction procedure has been used. The unstandardized ordinary least squares estimators, as well as the t-ratios, are presented in the table. Variables representing three phenomena meet the traditional .05 significance tests (a t-ratio of 1.69 is required, assuming a one-tail test and thirty-nine cases) -- salary increases, real income, and the presence or absence of a strict seniority system -- but the bulk of the explanatory power seems to be coming from the seniority variable. The variables for redistricting, pension, percent obedience to the seniority rule, and level of institutionalization are not statistically significant, and the latter is even in the unexpected direction.

Even though there are no difficuulties with autocorrelation, another common problem with regression equations -- multicollinearity -- is present. The problem is fairly easy to solve since in two instances, two variables measure the same or very similar phenomena. Both "dichotomized seniority" and "percent obedience to seniority" measure obedience to the seniority rule while both "salary increase" and "real salary" tap the monetary rewards of being a member of Congress. In this case we will drop the poorer predictors -- "percent obedience to seniority" and "real salary."[6]

When the regression equation is limited to the five remaining independent variables, autocorrelation does become a minor problem (D.W. of 1.6), so Cochrane-Orcutt autocorrelation correction procedures have been used. The results obtained by regressing these five independent variables on the number of retirements are presented in Table 1-7.

The equation presented in Table 1-7 is the preferred equation since it is relatively free from

Table 1-7

Regression of Voluntary Retirements on Five
Independent Variables, Correcting
for Autocorrelation

Variable	Coefficient	T-Ratio			
Redistirct- ing	1.50	.63	Constant	=	34.97
Salary Increase	- 4.99*	-2.15	R^2	=	.55
Pension Improvements	1.34	.42	D.W.	=	1.93
Dichotomized Seniority	-10.10*	-3.93	F	=	7.91
Institution- alization	- .12	- .84	N	=	38

the undesirable qualities sometimes present in regression equations. The level of multicollinearity among the independent variables[7] has been reduced by the omission of two variables[7] and the level of autocorrelation nearly disappears when the correlation is applied (D.W. of 1.93), although the correction has the undesirable side effects of reducing the number of cases by one and (usually) artificially inflating the R^2 (Kmenta, 1971).

Two of the variables in this preferred equation attain statistical significance -- dichotomized seniority and salary increases. By making a _ceteris_ _paribus_ assumption and by concentrating on the significant variables, we see that if there is no salary increase in a Congress and if the seniority rule is not an iron law, our model predicts there will be approximately 35 retirements (the constant). If, on the other hand, there is a salary increase and the seniority rule is nearly always followed, our model predicts there will be only about 20 retirements (34.97 - 4.99 - 10.10).

Thus, according to these equatioins, the number of voluntary retirements would be lowered by the institution of a strict seniority system and the granting of a salary increase. There is lesser and more unstable evidence that the number of retirees would be lowered by smaller pension annuities, an absence of upcoming redistrictings, and the existence of an institutionalized body (in the preferred equation the coefficient for institutionalization of the House has flipped over into the predicted direction, though it still does not come close to attaining statistical significance). The real value of computing equations in this situation is not in hoping we are able to predict the number of future retirees, but in seeing that our earlier discussions and speculations about the correlates of retirement are quite consistent with the results of these somewhat more rigorous procedures.

Conclusion

In this chapter I have attempted to determine the correlates of variations in the number of voluntary retirements from the House of Representatives. I have been especially sensitive to the ability of these variables to explain the recent increase in the number of retirements. To these ends, two variables proved most effective. First, the health of the seniority rule seemed to be the most promising variable. If the seniority rule is seldom violated in the selection of committeee chairmen, members are guaranteed committee chairs if they can stick around long enough; therefore, most of them do stick around so that they will be able to ascend to a position of power in the later stages of their careers. A second variable which seemed to be quite important was the monetary benefits of being a member of Congress. The value of the congressional salary (in real dollars) and especially the presence of a salary increase proved to be relatively accurate predictors of the number of voluntary retirements.

Several other variables seemed to be important only for portions of the twentieth-century: improvements in the pension annuities, redistricting, and the institutionalization of the House. Other variables -- trends in the society as a whole, and the degree of party competition for House seats -- were found to be largely inappropriate for one reason for another.

Of course, I have not considered all the possible causes of variations in the number of retirees. Many other factors, such as the large amount of mundane constituency service work modern representatives perform, have been proffered as reasons some members get out. But many of these variables suffer from the same problem which proved fatal to some variables contained in my analysis -- improper timing. The casework explanation provides a good example. The size of the bureaucracy and corresponding level of casework has grown steadily since the end of World War II (see Fiorina, 1977:54). However, the number of retirees has not grown steadily since 1945. Through the 1950s and 1960s the number of retirees declined while casework increased. Only in the 1970s have the two trends moved in tandem. Thus the overall match of the two trends is quite poor and certainly not supportive of the constituency service hypothesis. As we have seen, few variables, save for the seniority rule, make the requisite reversal in the early 1970s.

We might conclude that representatives, like most people, respond to monetary rewards and guaranteed positions of power. It would be surprising if they did not. However, one fairly important caution needs to be made about this conclusion and the chapter of which it is a part. Variations in the aggregate number of retirements and discussions of the variables which match these oscillations help to present the broader picture, but the desire to retire is an individual desire and is not effectively analyzed by looking only at the aggregate number of retirees per Congress. Fluctuations in overall numbers can only tell us so much about why individuals retire. To obtain the complete picture, aggregate data must be balanced with individual data; and what better place to obtain information on individual retirements than from the retirees themselves. In the next chapter I turn from an analysis of aggregate retirement levels to an analysis of the perceptions of individual voluntary retirees.

Footnotes

[1] For the record, the congressman is correct. The rate of retirement in the 1970s is not at all startling when compared to nineteenth-century retirement rates. Though data are hard to come by (most historical treatments rely on total turnover levels with little or no attention given to the makeup of that turnover), H. Douglas Price does report retirement figures for selected Congresses in the nineteenth-century. See Price, 1977:38. His figures show that in the selected Congresses the number who did not stand for re-election was indeed high by twentieth-century standards (although Price's figures do not allow us to separate those who ran for other office from those who retired from public service). See also Struble, 1979-80.

[2] Resignations are included here because they are a form of voluntary retirement. Resignations in recent years have been few in number and generally occur in the case of sudden illness or when a representative would not be counted as a retiree since there was no departure from public service. In the case of sudden illness, the resultant resignation would be counted as a voluntary retirement. Because the totals here include resignations as well as retirements, they will generally be slightly higher than the figures reported in "Congressional Quarterly's" computation of those who retired at the end of each Congress.

[3] A 1975 study by the Americans for Democratic Action determined that the benefits, salary, and allowances that go with a seat in Congress added up to about $500,000 per year.

[4] In the last year of the 91st Congress (1970), the mean number of years served by those in the House was nearly eleven. Throughout the 1970s, there was a steady drop in this figure. By 1980, the mean length of service for those in the House was under eight years. These figures represent the mean tenure of members in the second year of each Congress. Thus, someone who is first elected in 1958 has one year of tenure in the 86th Congress, according to the calculations made here. As a result, these figures may not be completely consistent with those tenure computations which are made at the beginning of each Congress.

[5]The R^2 may be slightly inflated in this situation due to the fact that we are using seven independent variables to "explain" only thirty-nine cases.

[6]I estimated the equation with "percent obedience to seniority" and "real salary" included and "salary increase" and "dichotomized seniority" excluded. "Percent obedience to seniority" and "real salary" were still not significant (.05) in this situation.

[7]After the removal of the two variables, a small degree of multicollinearity remained. The variable representing the institutionalization of the House is correlated with some of the other independent variables. The model was estimated without "institutionalization" and the coefficients and significance of the remaining variables changed barely at all. "Institutionalization" never attained significance (.05), even when tried as the lone independent variable. Thus, although some multicollinearity is present, it is not distorting the results. Outside of this variable, the level of multicollinearity was trivial.

CHAPTER TWO

I QUIT: THE COSTS OF CONGRESSIONAL SERVICE

The decision to retire is in the end an individual decision. Regardless of the amount of input supplied by family, friends, and close advisers, the congressman must at some point determine whether or not he wants to return to the halls of Congress for two more years. The only person in a position to know the factors which were crucial in the retirement decision is the retiree himself. Though I believe objective analysis of the patterns of voluntary retirement is vital, no thorough exploration of the topic is complete if it does not include the retirees' own account of the decision to quit. Their views on the nature of the job, and their perceptions of their own and their colleagues' reasons for leaving provide the necessary inside view of retirement motivations.

The Interviews

Some interviewing of recently retired members of Congress has been undertaken by other researchers -- usually members of the popular press (see, for example, O'Brien, 1978; Abramson, 1980; and Sinclair, 1980). A major drawback with these previous studies is that they generally rely on the comments of one, two, or at the most, three individuals. Often the retirees included were selected because they remained in the Washington-New York area after leaving Congress or because their retirements were perceived to have been "surprising" and were therefore deemed newsworthy, not because they were thought to be typical of the entire population of retirees.

Thanks to a grant from the National Science Foundation, I was able to interview twenty-four retirees rather than just one or two. I also was able to interview retirees who returned to Texas, California, or anywhere else upon their retirement rather than only those who stayed near the media centers. I selected as my target population the members of the 1978 House retirement class. I was able to conduct interviews with all but seven of the thirty-one members who voluntarily left the House in 1978. (Of the seven, two would not consent to an interview, one was seriously ill, one had an unobtainable mailing address, and three had schedules which made them unavailable at the time I was able to conduct the interview.) The interviews took place in the summer of 1980, about one and one-half years after the retirees left office. All were conducted by myself, and all but three were done in person. Due to scheduling conflicts, the three remaining interviews had to be done on the phone. The length of the interviews ranged from twenty minutes to nearly three hours. All were tape-recorded. Though a few did not insist on it, I have followed the practice of not identifying any of the retirees who made the statements presented here. As a result of these interviews, some general conclusions about the causes of voluntary retirement from the House can be drawn.

Like any other decision, whether or not to remain in the House can be seen as a cost-benefit problem. If the costs outweigh the benefits, the rational member will retire. If the benefits exceed the costs, the member will seek re-election. There are obvious benefits to be derived from serving in the House: a decent salary ($60,662), good job security (a 95 percent re-election rate), prestige, a modest degree of fame, and an opportunity to be close to the vortex of power. As one former member put it, "We are in a position where we can believe that we really make a difference." But there are also obvious costs: the job is extremely demanding; congressmen are constantly on the run; they are frequently away from their families; their performance is re-evaluated every two years; and they seldom feel they can really and truly relax. The most common theme I heard from the retirees was that though there have always been costs associated with congressional service, the costs of serving in the modern Congress are extraordinarily high. What follows is a description of these costs, as perceived by the retirees themselves.

Familial Sacrifices

One of the most common statements I heard was that raising a family and serving in Congress do not mix. Though for the most part members were reluctant to single out one reason as the most important cause of their retirement, several made it clear that their prime motivation in retiring was a desire to spend more time with their families.

One young retiree spoke for many when he said, "If I didn't enjoy my wife and kids, I would have stayed." Several retirees spoke wistfully about the events they were not able to share with their children. A veteran of many years in the House told me that during his entire career he was able to see only one of his son's little league baseball games, and he received a speeding ticket going to that one. Another told me about the time his son complained that he was the only boy in his class who had been taught to drive by his mother. A middle-aged, midwestern representative had a fairly vivid recollection of the events surrounding his realization that he was missing too much:

> I was back in the district watching somebody else's kid play soccer, presenting them with a flag or some such thing. I realized that I should have been watching my own kid play soccer. After all, that's what I really wanted to be doing.

Eighteen months later he retired.

Another set of comments displayed a concern with not being a proper parent. In defending his retirement decision, one said simply, "I decided to put my family first. They need me." One member who retired after a very brief stay in Washington said:

> My kids were getting ready to enter what I have always believed to be a very formative period. I did not want to jeopardize their welfare by not providing a good family environment during those critical years.

The Fishbowl Factor

What many members referred to as "the fishbowl factor" is another cost of serving in Congress. Congressmen and their families are scrutinized by media people as well as by constituents. As one California retiree told me, "People seem to feel public officials should not be allowed to have private lives." Nor surprisingly, this feeling of constantly being on display grates the nerves of many representatives.

Several retirees described specific instances of distasteful media activity. A southern member told me the following story:

> My wife and I built a home on a lake. The media people went out in a boat and took pictures of it under construction and put them in the Sunday paper along with how much I paid for the property and who I bought it from. They thought it was their right and maybe it is, but I don't think that is an acceptable way for people to behave.

A member who was in a somewhat ticklish position due to his duties in the House described what turned out to be an unpleasant week for him:

> We literally had platoons of reporters from the Washington Post, The Wall Street Journal, and all the state newspapers searching through court records and newspaper files, talking with people, doing anything they could to find someone or something that would say something unkind about me. They didn't have any luck, but I did not enjoy that experience in the slightest.

One member who was unmarried and supposedly "eligible" said:

> The camera has gone from Hollywood to Washington. Politics has replaced the world of entertainment. Every raise of the eybrow and every word is analyzed. I was paired off with everyone. I was offended to have the papers speculate about every person I would be seen with.

More often than not, however, the retirees I spoke with were critical of the media exposure because of what it did to their families. The following two quotes are typical of this feeling:

> You are bound to get unfavorable press sometime. I could handle it, but it

was hard for my family. I came home several times to find my wife in tears over what someone had written about me.

I think the fishbowl is harder on the family. It was hard for my kids to relax because they knew anything they did had the potential to affect my career. There is a different set of expectations for "the congressman's kids."

The exposure of the private lives of public officials is not entirely the result of the media. Several retirees told me that word-of-mouth gossip around the district is just as dangerous and annoying. An elderly retiree described the following events:

One night I went up to the grocery store to pick up some things. There was a kid I knew hanging around the store. It so happened that one of my purchases was a six-pack of beer. The next thing I knew the story was going around that I was dead drunk when I went into the grocery store. I hadn't had a drink to my name, but those are the things you have to expect when you are in the public eye.

There was a nearly universal feeling on the part of retirees that the scrutiny of public officials, whether by the media or constituents, is much too intense and that something needs to be changed in this area.

Ethics Provisions

The privacy of members of Congress is further jeopardized by the so-called ethics provisions, many of which were either enacted or tightened in the early 1970s. (See Congressional Quarterly, 1977, for a thorough description of these provisions as well as a history of their passage.) One of the most notable of these provisions requires members to make a public disclosure of their financial situation. Somewhat surprisingly, perhaps, the consensus of the retirees with whom I spoke was that, though this requirement was unnecessary and even repulsive, it was not an important cause of voluntary retirement.[1] This comment from a northeastern representative who retired in 1978 is fairly typical:

> Disclosure didn't cause me to leave but I do object to the requirement. Just because I am in public office, I do not have to give up all my privacy. I didn't mind it all that much, but I think it is absurd to say that my wife has to disclose all her holdings.

Another retiree had a slightly different reason for disliking the disclosure requirement:

> Disclosure didn't affect my decision, but it is affecting the kind of person who comes and stays in Congress. Disclosure encourages two types of people to enter Congress -- those who have no money and those who have only their daddy's money. It discriminates against successful businessmen -- those who have made moves and acquired wealth through their good business sense -- and these are the very people we need in Washington.

Despite a lot of complaining, few retirees said that financial disclosure was the reason they left.

Reaction to some of the other ethics provisions -- limits on honoraria and other outside income, for example, was largely the same. One fairly youthful retiree told me:

> The outside earnings limits are grossly unfair. I receive a great deal of my income from stocks and there are no limits on this type of income. But some of the members -- I can think of Otis Pike and Pat Moynihan in particular -- relied on giving speeches to make ends meet. Why should they be punished and not me?

But few retirees claimed they left because of the outside earnings limits.[2] All in all, the prevailing attitude toward the ethics provisions is best summed up by this comment from an elderly retiree:

I don't agree with all that crap. I am embarrassed when people find out how little I am worth, and I am disgusted when they tell me what speeches I can and cannot give, but they (the ethics provisions) were not factors in my decision to get out.

Constituency Service Work

It could reasonably be expected that the large amount of time devoted to "casework" would represent a disappointment to a legislator who came to Congress with hopes of tackling the great legislative issues of the day but finds instead that he spends most of his time on the phone to the Veterans Administration or trying to find lost social security checks. One former member expressed his disappointment this way: "All a member of Congress needs to do to win re-election is run a good public-relations opeation and answer his mail promptly. What kind of whore am I?" (Bethel, 1979). Thus, the much discussed ombudsman work of members of Congress (see Fiorina, 1977) may be a cause of voluntary retirements.

To be sure, there were some complaints about the number, manner, and appropriateness of constituent requests. Some retirees told me that constituents were increasingly caustic and demanding, while one relatively young retiree told the following story:

I remember one person who asked if I knew Judge So-And-So. I said that I did. He said, "Well, I've just been convicted of a crime and I was wondering if you could call the judge and ask him to give me the lightest possible sentence." I felt no embarrassment in telling him that what he was asking for was clearly improper and probably illegal. He became quite huffy, nor surprisingly, but he knew he was wrong.

But on the whole the retirees vigorously disagreed with the notion that the burgeoning number of constituent service chores was a factor in their decisions to retire. Many claimed these chores were actually enjoyable. For example, a sixty-two year old retiree who had served a district in the eastern part of the country told me:

The biggest satisfaction of the job is the opportunity to help the people. We were a service-oriented office, and I am proud of that. I could tell you some very heart-touching stories about the things we were able to do for some people. I loved that part of the job, and my staff was a great help.

An elderly, southern retiree had a slightly different reason for enjoying casework:

You learn more about the job by doing constituent service work than anything else. It shows you where the loopholes and cracks in the legislation are. It tells you whether or not the legislation is doing what it is supposed to do. It is avaluable learning experience, and it keeps you in touch with the people.

And an individual who retired after many years of service to his California district said:

I can see where you might think casework is not challenging, and in some ways it is not. But it _is_ rewarding. One of the pleasures of growing older was in knowing where to get quick cooperation for constituents and their problems. One quick phone call can do it. When I was younger, I would have had my staff chasing all over Washington.

But perhaps the most frequently cited reason for casework not being a cause of retirement was that the representative himself did not handle much of the casework. Retiree after retiree told about his or her great staff, and described to me how the staff was set up to handle constituent requests (most of which were pedestrian and easily handled by the staff). If the members did all the casework themselves, perhaps the high level of constituent service would be mentioned as a cause for leaving, but since most members farmed these tasks out to their staffs, the general feeling was that service work was not driving numerous representatives from the Congress.

If this <u>had</u> been a motivation, there would have been a lot of disappointment with the life of a retiree, because an end to constituent service work does <u>not</u> come with an end to congressional service. One retiree told me:

> That phone must ring at least half a dozen times a day, and it is always someone who either is having trouble with the bureaucracy or who needs information about the laws or the government.

I have no difficulty believing this to be true since several of my interviews with the retirees were interrupted by calls of this nature.

Disrespect for Public Officials

Another unpleasant fact of modern congressional life is the attitude of the public toward Congress and its members. Politics and politicians are not given a place of respect in the current public mood. Some retirees perceive the present public attitude as part of a "post-Watergate morality," but most feel the tendency to look askance at the political arena started long before Watergate. Regardless of when the trend started, several former members mentioned it as a contributing factor in their retirement decisions.

Many noted the public's disaffection is seldom directed at their own congressman, but is usually a more general disapproval of Congress as a whole (see Fenno, 1975). Even so, the assumption that all politicians are suspect makes the job less pleasant. One member who retired after serving six terms said:

> People just presume we are dishonorable. I don't know if you have ever been suspected of doing something dishonest, but if you have you know it is not a pleasant feeling until you are cleared. Well imagine living under a cloud of suspicion all the time. If you can do that, you can understand why some of us think serving in Congress isn't enjoyable.

A representative who retired after just a few years apparently was in office long enough to feel the public's disrespect:

> The vilification of the average politician in the eyes of the public is a very alarming trend. It makes it less pleasant for us to go out in public. We all like to be proud of the work we do, but some people seem to think I should be ashamed to have serviced in the U.S. Congress.

Thus, an additional cost of serving is produced by the less-than-respectful eyes with which much of the public looks upon Congress.

Interest Groups

The 1978 House retirees are in essential agreement regarding their attitude toward interest groups. Traditional interest groups are not viewed as troublesome. Witness the following two statements:

> Lobbyists were no problem. I used them, in fact, to enlarge my staff. If there was going to be a labor bill on the floor, I would write to the AFL-CIO and ask why I should vote labor on the issue. Then I would send their response to the National Association of Manufacturers and ask them to rebut the arguments of the AFL-CIO. It saved work for the staff, and it was an effective way of separating the wheat from the chaff in the respective arguments.
>
> I felt I had a very straightforward relationship with the various lobbies. They were honest with me, perhaps because they knew I wouldn't take any crap. I even initiated a sign-in procedure in my office for anyone who was not a constituent. It worked very well and there were surprisingly few complaints.

But there was universal condemnation of the growing number of single-issue interest groups:

...Now the single-issue people are something else again. I have no time for them. There are no shades of support -- just black and white. That is a very irrational outlook and I'm sorry to see it proliferate. They have one question and if you're not "right" on it, that's it. They don't care about anything else.

Two things combined to cause me to leave Congress, and the proliferation and growing power of single-issue groups is one of them. They are ruining Congress, or I should say, the members are letting them ruin Congress.

The rise of these groups should not be discounted as an important contributing factor in the general dissatisfaction with the life of a representative and the resultant high retirement rate.

Lack of Security

The job of a representative has unusual requirements. One requirement is that after every two years the relevant public passes judgment on the performance of each representative. This situation sets the job apart from most, and the knowledge that "the axe can fall" at any time can be psychologically costly. A California retiree said:

Every time you turn around there is another election coming up. It makes things more intense and nerve-wracking. You are always running and I suspect this is why members of the House seem to burn out more quickly than senators. I suppose I would still be there if I didn't have to run for re-election every two years.

Many observers assume that in recent years electoral costs have been minimal since most representatives win re-election by lopsided margins (see Mayhew, 1974). But as Thomas Mann (1978) has pointed out, feelings of insecurity may not be related to actual victory margin. Though many of the retirees I spoke with were reluctant to admit to any electoral fears, after some prodding, concern over the outcome of the frequent elections became obvious. The following two statements are illustrative:

> Wondering when the axe is going to fall is no fun. There is a volatility in recent elections that is disconcerting. I went from 69 percent to 51 percent in the space of two years. I knew that if my party had a bad year it would be all over for me. It's frustrating to know that so much of the outcome is out of your hands.

> A couple of my friends got beaten for absolutely no reason. That's always the way it is, every election there are a few defeats that are completely unpredictable. It makes you wonder when it will happen to you. It makes things nerve-wracking, and I suspect it is why members of the House burn out more quickly than senators.

Though it is quite unlikely that electoral concerns could explain the <u>increase</u> in voluntary retirements (since House members are objectively safer now than they used to be and since the term has always been two years long), they are still an important and frequently mentioned cost of serving in the House.

Campaigning and Fundraising

The two-year term creates other costs in addition to general insecurity. Members are forced to campaign and raise needed funds almost constantly. Campaigning is not a major cost of the job: many retirees even voiced a liking for campaign activities. But fundraising is a different matter. Several representatives stated that fundraising is easily the most distasteful aspect of the job. Apparently, its distasteful nature does not diminish with time, as the comments of this veteran of over twenty-five years in the House make evident:

> The thing I hated most of all was fundraising. Campaigning actually can be fun once you get in the swing of things, but I never enjoyed fundraising -- not for one minute -- and I was good at it. It's degrading for my friends

and also for myself, and it's becoming more and more important. If I could put my finger on one thing that drove me out of office, it would be fund-raising.

A much more youthful retiree had this to say about modern fundraising:

The amount of money needed for a viable campaign in this day and age is out-rageous. You have to raise money constantly and this is a big nuisance, especially for the older members because they are not used to it. But even if you are young, fundraising is nothing but hard work. I don't know anyone who enjoys it. By the way I still owe from my last campaign. If you have some loose change...

Fundraising constitutes a very important cost of congressional service in the minds of the retirees with whom I spoke.

Low Salary

In documenting the costs of serving in the House, we must recognize the fact that by being in Congress members are foregoing the opportunity to do something else. In cost-benefit analysis it is necessary to consider in the cost tabulation the benefits that are forfeited by the selection of one particular option. In deciding whether or not to retire, members compare the costs and benefits of continuing in Congress with the costs and benefits of returning to the practice of law, for example. Thus, before we conclude this treatment of the costs of congressional service, we must give some considera-tion to the costs of not receiving the benefits of doing something else.

These opportunity costs (sometimes referred to as foregone benefits) can be seen most clearly in the area of salary. The salary of $60,662 that congress-men receive is a benefit. The salary that could be received in other lines of work is a cost. And for many members the forfeited salary is quite large. The congressional salary has not been able to keep pace with private sector salaries. In fact, it has not even come close. One young retiree said simply, "Private industry salaries are so much higher it is ridiculous." An elderly member who retired to his Texas district in 1978 described the reversal he witnessed over the course of his long career:

> The relationship of the congressional salary to private industry salaries has done a reversal. When I entered Congress, the salary was $10,000. At that time there weren't but two or three lawyers in all of my hometown making $10,000. Now the salary is $60,000, but there must be two-hundred lawyers in this town making that, maybe more.

Another retiree, this one from the eastern part of the country, said:

> One of the important reasons I got out was that I wanted to build some estate for my family before I was too old. The congressional salary kept food on the table, but it did not make me a rich man. Private industry salaries are much higher.

Several retirees told me their net worth actually decreased while they were in Congress. All of them agreed they could have done beter financially if they had never run for Congress.

Former members of Congress are very desirable commodities for private industry employers. I asked the retirees why this was so, and the following reasons were frequently given. First, the modern Congress, through its committee structure, allows and in fact encourages representatives to specialize in certain areas. Once the retirement decision is announced, private industries relevant to the member's area(s) of expertise see an opportunity to obtain some valuable knowledge and experience (see Sinclair, 1980). A second reason is that as the government becomes involved in more things, there is a greater premium placed on understanding the rules and regulations of the government. This fact is evident in the burgeoning number of industries and law firms that are opening Washington offices. What better place to get knowledge of governmental activities than from someone who had a hand in formulating the rules and is familiar with the Washington terrain? Third, the drawing power of a former member of Congress can probably bring in additional clients to law firms and the like. Finally, former members of Congress have a ready set of contacts on the Hill. They even enjoy some privileges (such as access to members while they are on the floor of the House) other lobbyists do not (see Keller, 1980). When all these things are combined, it is not surprising that employers from the private sector are very eager to secure the services of a former member of Congress.

This eagerness is evident in both the quantity and quality of offers made to members who announce their retirements. One of the better-known members of the 1978 retirement class told me:

> I don't mean to blow my own horn, but after I announced my retirement I must have heard from every major law firm in the country. Some of the offers were generous beyond my expectations. I took the best one.

Another retiree decided to turn down many lucrative offers and return to his home in California. He said:

> I suppose I had the same kinds of offers that are made to anyone who has been in Washington a long time and who has written a lot of law. I could have stayed in Washington and become a very rich man.

With very generous offers waiting in the wings, the indirect salary costs of serving in the House are extremely high. The combination of better pay and fewer hours creates an irresistable temptation for many members.

The Congressional Pension

There is an additional foregone benefit which contributes to the temptation to leave Congress -- the lucrative congressional pension plan. In discussing the pension many retirees were reluctant to attribute it much importance in the decision to retire. Nonetheless, most retirees -- especially those who had logged a good deal of time in Congress

-- acknowledged the pension as a contributing factor. One told me:

> It's hard to say how much of a part the pension played. There's no denying it was involved. It made the decision easier. It's a liberal plan and now that we are back home where the cost of living is reasonable it looks even better.

In considering the role of the pension plan in voluntary retirement from Congress one must remember that, though the retirements of members with many years of service are encouraged, the retirement decisions of younger members are discouraged since they stand to lose a substantial amount of potential pension money due to their truncated service. More will be said about this situation in Chapter 3.

Legislative Frustrations

One reason to resist the temptation offered by such things as the attractive private sector jobs and the lucrative pension is the opportunity for members of Congress to leave a mark on legislation, thereby improving the lot of the country and constituents. As one former member put it, there is the chance "to do good." As we shall see shortly, however, there is a widespread belief that the present legislative situation makes it difficult to influence public policy. In fact, some see the legislative situation as a cost and not a benefit of congressional service.

One very senior member had this to say about the rewards of serving in Congress:

> Of course members aren't being paid enough. You can't pay members of Congress in proportion to the importance of their position. A large part of the compensation <u>has</u> to come in the satisfaction of doing the job -- the intangibles of holding office, making good policy and serving the country.

But many retirees describe the modern Congress as a place in which there is little opportunity to leave a real mark on important, new legislation and, consequently, as a place in which it is difficult to take pride in the intangibles. Though one goal of the 1970s House reforms was to broaden representation by getting more legislators involved in the process, many 1978 retirees feel the House has been brought to a virtual standstill by, among other things, these procedural reforms and the perceived over de-centralization which resulted. The legislative process, instead of providing intangible rewards, is providing frustrations. Instead of the ability "to do good" being a motivation to stay in, the perceived legislative deadlock has become a reason to get out. A sixty-one year old retiree told me, "I got out because I wanted to get something done. There is no opportunity in the House to get things done anymore."

Several members spoke longingly of the 1960s, when streams of important legislation flowed from Congress. By way of contrast, many said that in the 1970s all they were doing was "finetuning" previously passed legislation and checking up on executive agencies. Important work, I was told, but seldom satisfying work. There was a strong feeling that the reforms had fractionalized the process and made it more difficult to pass important new legislation. Too often upon introduction such legislation would be carved up, sent to countless subcommittees, and never seen again.

Thus, many see the time spent in the modern post-reform House as wasted time -- as time that could be spent doing something more productive -- as an opportunity cost. But what brought about this unpleasant legislative situation? What are the specific sources of this cost? Several factors were frequently mentioned by the 1978 retirees.

Trivial Roll Call Votes

The high number of trivial roll call votes -- quorum calls, votes on motions to approve the journal, and other unimportant matters -- is one of the most bothersome traits of the modern House. Many retirees voiced objections to the practice of using roll call votes as dilatory tactics. A member who retired at about age sixty said, "Congress is immobilized. No policy is coming out, and part of the reason is the time wasted on quorum calls and the like." Another told me that he "sensed a growing anger with the procedural foolishness -- especially the number of wasted trips to the floor in order to make a quorum call." And a third made reference to the king of dilatory tactics, former representative H.R. Gross (R.-Iowa).

> I grudgingly respected H.R. Gross and his dilatory tactics. He knew the issues, he was always prepared, and he had an amazing command of parliamentary procedure. Well, the number of people who want to slow the House down has proliferated, but none of them have the skill of Mr. Gross. They are bringing the House to a standstill and they are frustrating most of the members.

In addition a young retiree voiced his frustration with a type of vote he views as no better than a quorum call:

> I heard a lot of complaining about the number of quorum calls, but my biggest gripe was with the ceremonial stuff we got involved in. I routinely voted against this kind of legislation -- all of it. I remember one time we voted on a motion to make the square-dance the national dance. I caught up with the person who introduced the motion and asked him why he had made a motion to make the square-dance the national dance. He looked at me, and I think his response summed up the prevailing philosophy of the members when he said, "because that's what a lot of my people think it should be." Well I don't care what the people of his district think about the square-dance, the Congress has more important things to do.

Whether it is a quorum call or a vote to make the square-dance the national dance, many members feel a lot of valuable time is wasted because of the large number of trivial roll call votes.

Changes in the Committee System

Another source of great frustration for some members is the reforms in the committee system which occurred in the 1970s. I heard numerous complaints about the proliferation of subcommittees, the weakening of committee chairmen, the open-to-the-public

executive committee sessions,[3] and the scheduling
of committee meetings;[4] but the most frequently
criticized change proved to be the decline in the
seniority rule as a criterion for the selection of
committee chairmen (for a description of these
changes, see Chapter 1). Many retirees felt the
changes in the processs of selecting committee chairmen were quite detrimental to the legislative
process. One member used the situation of W.R. (Bob)
Poage (D.-Texas) -- long-time chairman of the House
Agriculture Committee who was deposed as chairman in
1975 despite his satus as the most senior majority
member on the committee -- as an example:

> Some of the actions of these reformers
> were clearly out of line, and I am
> thinking especially of what they did to
> Bob Poage. They were just out for
> blood and Bob was handy. Men who voted
> against him were ashamed of it later
> because Bob was a perfect gentleman and
> an outstanding chairman.

One of the 1978 retirees had been a victim of
the 1975 "coups" against the seniority rule. He was,
however, very understanding of the pressures on those
who acted against him:

> Those young fellas got in by promising
> to clean up the system. Once they were
> in, they had to make good on those prom-
> ises. I don't fault them for that.

But this former member, like the clear majority of
1978 retirees, spoke very critically of some of the
consequences of the new selection procedures:

> Here is what happens with the new
> system, if you can call it that.
> Fellas who should be backing my succes-
> sor (as committee chairmen) are under-
> cutting him -- undercutting him because
> they want to get rid of him so they can
> get up there. Now, that is a bad
> system when you have the members of a
> committee all running around to take
> the chairman's place, trying to oust
> him. It keeps the system from working.
> They are competing when they should be
> cooperating. I felt this a little
> before I left, and at times I was more

> comfortable with members from the other
> side of the aisle (Republicans) -- at
> least I didn't have questions about
> their motives.

Support for the concept of seniority was wide-spread -- one member even told me, "the only thing wrong with seniority is that I never had enough of it" -- although not unanimous. But regardless of their feelings toward the decreased value of seniority, all believed this decrease was an important reason for the increase in the number of voluntary retirements. To some extent this increase would be a direct response to a devaluation of long tenure (if the rewards of staying a long time are reduced, it is not surprising fewer people choose to stay a long time), but the changes in the seniority rule could also be connected to the increase in voluntary retirements because they, like many of the other reforms, adversely affected the legislative process (according to the retirees with whom I spoke). A closer analysis of the seniority explanation is provided in the next chapter.

A New Type of Member

A third major source of trouble for the legislative process in the House, according to the retirees, is the behavior of those who have been recently elected to Congress. Many retirees believe this new generation is different from older generations, and most see it as a change for the worse. The perception that, as one member told me, "there is a new breed of cat," is common.

Many of the negative comments focused on the large entering class of 1975, but there was also a general dissatisfaction with the priorities and styles of all new members. Said one older retiree:

> Today it is all publicity. These young
> guys play to the public and to tele-
> vision. They're all in it for them-
> selves, and most of them are damned
> hard to work with.

Other comments on this supposedly uncooperative style of many of the new members included the following quotes:

When I came here, most of the men who served were men of substance. In the old days they did what they thought was best. Today most are fellas who won a big murder case or something and got a lot of publicity. They don't do what they think is best; they just try to imagine how each vote is going to sound.

In Congress today there are far too many people who are more interested in the most recent poll than in their own principles. Most of them posture the whole time. They give the same speeches on the floor as they give to the Rotary Club back home. We don't want to hear those speeches; we give them ourselves. These people have nothing to contribute to the process.

Not surprisingly, the older retirees were more critical of the new style of member than were the younger retirees. The picture painted by the older retirees was that their own generation was hard-working, legislatively astute, and willing to do the necessary behind-the-scenes work, while the new generation tended to be composed of showy, public-relations oriented posturers who lacked the desire and savvy needed to make real contributions to leislation. Younger retirees, of course, were not as likely to criticize the generation to which they belong, although there were many young retirees who agreed that on the whole their generation was more self-centered and publicity conscious.

Unfortunately, it is impossible to determine how much of this talk about an undesirable new breed of cat can be attributed to an endemic tendency of previous generations to criticize those that follow and how much stems from a real change in the type of individual who enters Congress. The fact that some of the younger members are critical of their own generation indicates that there is probably at least some truth to the "new type of member" claims.[5] The important point, however, is that many members perceive that one of the reasons for the stagnated legislative process is an uncooperative and media-oriented new generation of representative.

Over De-Centralization

These three factors -- an increase in the number of trivial roll call votes, various alterations in the committee system, and an influx of uncooperative new members -- are what the retirees believe to be the major causes of a fractionalized and largely untenable legislative situation. Several retirees spoke of a "general lack of collegiality." One older member described it this way:

> The lack of a willingness to cooperate is the hallmark of the modern House. (Former Speaker) Sam Rayburn was a benevolent dictator. He was a great man and a great American, but I don't think even Sam could control that bunch they have in there now. It's a mess and it's impossible to get things done.

Similar comments were frequently made during the interviews. For example, a middle-aged representative who retired to his California district in 1978 said:

> The House has democratized and decentralized to the point of ridiculousness. The leadership is helpless and all anyone worries about is the next election. There is too much backbiting. Disputes in the House used to be political; now they frequently turn personal. What we are left with is quite an unpleasant parliamentary situation. There is no sense of togetherness or direction.

As a result of the fractionalized legislative situation, many of the retirees felt they were "spinning their wheels" in the House. Thus, legislative frustration increases the opportunity costs (foregone benefits) and is an important cause of many voluntary retirements.

Miscellaneous Comments on Retirement

In addition to the factors mentioned in the previous pages, the retirees made several comments to me which, although informative, do not fall into any of the categories I have used to organize this chapter. What follows is a quick sampling of these comments.

One frequent comment was that some members stay too long. I heard several horror stories about elderly members who became embarrassments. For example:

> Manny Celler was an amazing man. He was serving in the House before I was born, and when I arrived he was sharp as a tack. When he rose to speak, he commanded attention because people knew he had something to say. But Manny didn't know when to quit. He stayed too long and everyone could see him slipping mentally. But your friends don't tell you that. When I saw this happen I vowed I would never let it happen to me.

Several others said that when they entered the House (or maybe even before) they decided to serve only a set period of time. One youthful retiree said:

> I went in firm in the belief that I would not make Congress a career. Ten to twelve years is enough for anyone. Though I do not favor a mandatory term limit, I think it is bad for Congress and the country when members serve for extended periods of time.

Finally, in attempting to explain the large increase in the number of retirees some members suggested there may be a sort of contagion effect. One young retiree whose announcement caused a great deal of surprise and media attention told me he was swamped by fellow members the day after a television show featured an interview with him.

> All kinds of members from both sides of the aisle told me that they were thinking about getting out and that they agreed with all the things I said about the job. One member said he and his wife had been talking about retiring for many years and that after they saw the piece on me they decided to actually go through with it."

Another retiree said that whenever he returns to Washington current members converge on him and ask all kinds of questions about retirement. "I tell them I've never been happier and my golf handicap has been lowered by five. I recommend retirement to anyone who has any doubts at all about the job."

Conclusion

To be sure, some retirements result from idiosyncratic factors -- health, scandal or some unusual personal situation, just to name a few. There is even the case of a member of Congress who retired not because he was denied a chairmanship, but because he was <u>granted</u> a committee chairmanship. Those close to him claimed he was scared to death of being in charge of an entire committee. No study could document all the reasons for leaving Congress. Nonetheless on many points there was surprising consensus among the retirees I interviewed. There was widespread agreement on the undesirability of many of the elements of modern congressional life. There also was widespread agreement among the two dozen retirees that the costs of congressional service have gone up dramatically in recent years. It is these costs that, in the words of one retiree, lead members:

> ...to want to go home, put their feet up, take the phone off the hook, sleep late, and tell people to go to hell when they deserve to be told that.

[1]Since all the retirees I spoke with retired in 1978, they had all been forced to disclose in previous years. Given this fact, it would have been surprising if financial disclosure requirements had forced them to leave. If the members felt these requirements were so objectionable, they probably would have retired earlier -- perhaps before they ever had to disclose. While disclosure may have been the cause of some retirements earlier in the 1970s (immediately after enactment), the retirees of 1978 did not see it as an important cause of their retirement decisions.

[2]In 1981 these limits were lifted for senators. They remain in place for members of the House of Representatives, although they now are less stringent.

[3]One member said:

> Executive sessions of committees should not be opened to the public. Once you do this, what happens? The only people sitting out there looking at you are the damned lobbyists. You can't speak your mind. When you open it up, you really don't open it up to the public. Some members show off to the lobbyists. When you had men of honor serving on committees and when you had closed sessions, you could get things done.

[4]The following quote is a good example of the complaints I heard about the scheduling of committee meetings:

> I have a couple of complaints about the committee system. First, we have too many assignments. It even took my secretary a couple of weeks to understand the way things work. I would have subcommittee meetings starting at 9:00, 9:30, and 10:00. She thought that one was done before the other started, so she was trying to schedule things in between. I had to explain to her that each meeting ran til 1:00. So even the staff loses perspective of the

demands and overlap of committees. Also, the hearings are way too redundant. We usually get eight or nine statements, all a couple of inches thick and all saying very nearly the same thing.

[5]Also on this point, see the work of James Payne (1980).

CHAPTER 3

WHO QUITS

In the last two chapters, different questions have been posed and different types of data employed. In the first chapter, aggregate data were used to determine why the number of retirees waxed and waned in the particular pattern it did. In the second chapter, systematic interview data were used to find out why recent retirees decided to leave the House. In the current chapter, I take yet another approach to the issue of voluntary retirement. Here the question becomes why some members retire voluntarily and others do not. To answer this question, I will attempt to determine the personal qualities or situations which seem to predispose members to retire. This exercise will assist us greatly in drawing conclusions about the causes of voluntary retirement. In order to explore the issue, I will employ objective individual level data for all the members of ten recent Congresses. By comparing the traits of those who did retire with those who did not, we will be able to make inferences about the factors which influence members to retire voluntarily.

This chapter can be placed with a group of studies that has grown out of ambition theory. Usually these studies trace their roots to Joseph Schlesinger's _Ambition and Politics_ (1966). Schlesinger's ambition theory rests on the assumption that _the behavior of political office-holders is partially dependent upon the ambition of those office-holders_. The ambition of office-holders thus becomes a topic of utmost importance.

Schlesinger procedes to a threefold classification of ambition. A politician who wants to serve the remainder of the present term before withdrawing from elective office is said to possess _discrete_ ambition; one who wishes to make a long-run career of the present position has _static_ ambition; and a politician who aspires to an office more important than the one presently held is said to have _progressive_ ambition (1966:10).

It is frequently assumed that all members of Congress possess static ambition. David Mayhew's essay _Congress: The Electoral Connection_ is based on the notion that every representative is driven by the desire to be re-elected. Schlesinger himself states that:

> The congressman...is in a position which combines intrinsic satisfactions with the possibilities of long tenure; we would expect such a position to foster static ambitions (1966:11).

It is also quite common to assume that progressive ambition is prevalent among politicians. David Rohde, for example, claims that members of the House long to be a senator or a governor, but fail to try more often for these offices because of fears of defeat (1979).

All in all, it is not surprising that politicians have static or progressive ambitions -- it is what we would expect of people who are motivated to become politicians. Frank Kent once wrote that leaving political office "is never in the least voluntary...Every man who has held elective office wants to keep it or get a better one" (1936:177). Few are shocked when a politician announces an upcoming bid for higher office, and an announcement that an incumbent congressman is seeking re-election generally is cause for nothing more than a yawn. But when we hear of a politician who wants out of public service completely, questions immediately arise. With progressive and static ambition thought to be the norms among members of Congress, the existence of discrete ambition is something of a puzzle. Why do these people want to leave an office which, according to most observers, is the kind of position in which most people would want to stay?

Literature Review

For a time, the attention of researchers seemed to be directed at progressive ambition, perhaps reflecting the fact that Schlesinger's work dealt primarily with those who wanted to move up the political ladder (see Frost, 1972; Kritzer, 1978; and Rohde, 1979). Articles on voluntary retirement (discrete ambition) could be found only in the popular press. Recently, however, attention to House voluntary retirements has picked up. Stephen Frantzich addressed the general notion of voluntary retirement in two 1978 articles (1978a and 1978b),

Joseph Cooper and William West published two articles in 1981 on the topic (1981a and 1981b), and Albert Cover has also contributed a manuscript which documents and attempts to explain the growth in the number of House retirements.

These five studies of voluntary retirement are similar in several regards. All begin with discussions of what the authors term "traditional" explanations for retirement -- age, electoral vulnerability, and ambition. In each of the studies, these traditional explanations are found lacking. Thus the authors are forced to look elsewhere in their quest to explain voluntary retirements. The explanation settled upon in all cases (though with less enthusiasm by Cover) is that members of Congress are disaffected with modern congressional life.

As Chapter 2 demonstrated, it is indisputable that many current and recently retired members of Congress are disaffected with some aspects of congressional life. Nonetheless, the disaffection argument is in some ways unsatisfying. Saying that members of Congress leave because the House is not the kind of place in which they want to stay is not saying much at all. Further, the emergence of many of the trevails of modern congressional service is not consistent with the timing of the increase in voluntary retirements. The increase in constituent service work, for example, has been a gradual, long-term trend whereas the increase in retirements was sudden (the big increase came in 1972 at the end of the 92nd Congress) and has since leveled off (see Table 1-1), a poor match with the trend in service work. In addition, if disaffection is so widespread, why do approximately 400 of the 435 incumbents still seek re-election every two years? The goal of this study is to improve upon previous explanations of voluntary retirement from the House by determining the type of individual who is disaffected enough to get out.

The Study

Two reminders need to be made before I describe the specific procedures employed in this study. First, the phenomenon of interest is what Schlesinger calls discrete ambition and what I call voluntary retirement. This category includes members of the House who voluntarily retire for reasons other than a desire to enter or run for other public office. This definition is consistent with Frantzich's (1978a:253), however Cooper and West as well as Cover lump those with progressive ambition in with those who display discrete ambition. While progressive ambition is certainly an important research topic, it is quite a different thing from discrete ambition. Conceptual problems are created when these two groups are combined. For example, since many of the elements thought to influence a desire to leave the House (an inadequate salary and a more than adequate pension, to name just two) are the same in the Senate as they are in the House, why would anyone motivated by these factors leave the House and attempt to enter the Senate -- the body to which most representatives with progressive ambition aspire? Given the complicating factors, it seems logical to study discrete ambition separately from progressive ambition.

The second reminder is that the primary goal of this study is not an explanation of the increase in voluntary retirements, but an explanation of the kind of representative who was most likely to retire during the time period under study. Explanations of an over-time change in the number of retirees is best left to a time-series design such as that used in Chapter 1. In this chapter I am primarily interested in the general causes of voluntary retirement. The conclusions drawn may or may not be relevant to attempts to explain the increase in retirements. This potential relevance to the trend in voluntary retirements will be explored briefly in the third section of this chapter, but the two primary objectives are (1) to identify the variables which seem to be related to a tendency to retire voluntarily, and (2) to determine whether or not the power of these variables changed from the 1960s to the 1970s. As will be seen shortly, this second objective is crucial since it may be that there has been a change in the nature of voluntary retirements in addition to the previously documented change in the number of retirements. In other words, the reasons members retire may have changed. This is an issue which has received insufficient attention in previous research.

The period covered by this study runs from 1959 to 1978, thereby including ten Congresses. Personal data have been recorded[1] for the 435 members of each of the ten Congresses. This personal information includes age, entry age, seniority rank, previous occupation, party affiliation, party unity scores, conservative coalition scores, and the percent of the two-party vote received in the previous two elections. All these variables will be used in attempts to locate the kind of member who is most likely to retire at the end of the relevant Congress. I will also make extensive use of the interviews to assist in explaining hypotheses and findings.

In order to determine the ability of the coded variables to predict retirements, I have employed discriminant function analysis. Regression is made inappropriate because the dependent variable in the study is dichotomous (retire or not retire). When this is the case, one of the assumptions of regression is violated since the error term will not be normally distributed. Despite this, regression (either ordinary least squares, logit, or probit) is often used in such situations (see Gillespie, 1977, for a good comparison of these various techniques). However, in this study the dependent variable is not only dichotomous, it is badly skewed (212 cases of retire, 4,324 cases of not retire). In this situation, regression should not be used (see Kort, 1973 and Gillespie, 1977). Though regression is not appropriate, discriminant function analysis is ideally suited for the problem at hand (Kort, 1973 and Klecka, 1980). With discriminant function analysis the issue becomes how well each independent variable can discriminate between the two groups (retire and not retire). The standardized coefficients which result from discriminant function analysis can be interpreted in the same manner as standardized regression coefficients are interpreted. By entering all the variables simultaneously, the resultant coefficients represent the discriminating power of each variable with all other variables in the equation controlled. In addition, simultaneous entry removes the bias against late entering variables which is present in most stepwise techniques.

The Hypotheses

On the basis of past literature, common sense, and my discussions with the retirees, several expectations regarding the retirement tendencies of certain groups of representatives can be put forward. Elderly members, for example, should be more prone to retire than younger members. As ambition lessens and faculties slow, it is reasonable to expect that an increasing number of members will want to retire from the widely discussed rigors of public life. One retiree put it simply:

> There is no big mystery to my retirement. I was 74 and not in the best of health. The Congress is not a place for the enfeebled. It's a demanding job and I didn't want to stay too long, as a few of my dear friends did.

Once age is controlled, we could also reasonably expect seniority rank to be positively associated with voluntary retirement. Since it seems safe to assume one of the main motivations of members of Congress is the desire to maximize power within the House (see Fenno, 1973:3), and since seniority, for a large share of the period covered by this study, was an accurate predictor of power in the House, it makes sense to expect that, other things being equal, someone lacking in seniority should be more likely to retire than someone with a good deal of seniority. As one former member said to me:

> I thought quite a lot about retiring until I began to move up the ladder. Once I had my subcommittee chair those thoughts became very rare. When I became chairman of the full committee, they stopped altogether. I didn't want to give all that up.

For at least two reasons, membership in the minority party, which for the entire twenty-year period under study was the Republican party, should predispose an individual to retire. One reason for this expectation stems from the ideological frustration felt by many Republicans as they watched the Democratic majority preside over the growth of the federal government in the 1960s and 1970s. One Republican who was anything but elderly when he retired in 1978 told me, "I didn't like the direction the country was going in. I hadn't been effective in changing that direction so I quit fighting the big-spending liberals." Most Republicans were well aware that they were going to be on the losing end of most political battles, as the following comment illustrates: "Occasionally we Republicans could scrape together some kind of coalition, but not very often. I finally got tired of being in the back of the bus all the time."

Another potential source of minority party frustration derives from the procedures used in distributing the power positions in the House -- specifically the allocation of committee and subcommittee chairmanships. Even the most senior Republicans are blocked from these chairmanships because the majority party always places its own in these positions. There are several reasons to believe being blocked from the chairmanship of committees and subcommittees can make serving in the House less enjoyable. In general, the chairman is free to treat minority party members as second-class citizens. One Republican, for example, spoke of the frustration which comes when ideas are coopted by a committee chairman:

> I submitted a bill one time and the chairman said, "that's a damn good idea. How would you like me to reintroduce this as my bill, and you can put your name on it, too?" I said, "I wouldn't like that in the least because it's my bill." He said, "it will never get out of this committee if it's your bill. It will if it's mine." What could I do but curse under my breath and wish that just for one day I could be the chairman of a committee he was on?

Both ideological frustration and the frustration of being blocked from key committee positions lead us to expect members of the minority to be more likely to retire, but an important caution is in order. If ideological frustration influences retirement, this relationship should be evident among Democrats as well as Republicans. Many Democrats during the 1960s and 1970s -- particularly those from the South -- were in the partisan majority but the ideological minority. The following comments were made by a southern Democrat who retired in 1978:

> People with my views are gradually losing power in Congress. I couldn't stop a dangerous movement toward a welfare state with inadequate defenses. Every election brings more liberals and more free-spending.

Note the similarity of these comments to those made earlier by a Republican. Several other conservative Democrats expressed comparable feelings.

Observing the different retirement rates of Democrats and Republicans is not a very effective way of testing the role ideological frustration plays in retirement decisions. Thus, two alternative procedures will be used here. First, since most conservative Democrats are from the South, the tendency of southern Democrats to retire will be observed independently. The second and preferable method is to include in the multivariate model a variable which taps ideological position; therefore, I have included each member's rating on the conservative coalition scale as a variable.[2] The expectation is that because of the prevailing liberal sentiment in Congress during the 1960s and 1970s, conservatives felt out of step, and this feeling led an inordinate number of them to retire voluntarily. If being a Republican has an effect independent of ideological position, we will be able to conclude that the frustration which results from being denied committee chairmanships plays a role in the higher rate of Republican retirements.

The degree of electoral competition in the district is another variable which might be expected to influence retirement decisions. Though members of Congress, regardless of past victory margin, seem to feel some electoral worries (see Mann, 1978), for those serving a marginal district the insecurity is often especially intense. It is reasonable to expect that the pleasure of serving is diminished by the specter of defeat. This rationale is evident in the comments of a member who retired in 1978 at the age of 45: "I was in a very competitive district, and yes that helped me make the decision to get out. It makes serving much more difficult. The compromises I had to make in time and principles were more than I was willing to make."

The measure of electoral insecurity used here is the percent of the two-party vote received by the member in the last election.[3] This measure, of course, is not a perfect reflection of each member's electoral insecurities, but it seems to be the best measure available.[4]

The final variable to be tested is the degree to which members feel in line with their party. The thinking here is that mavericks -- those who feel out of step with the rest of the party -- will be more prone to retire than those who feel quite comfortable with the party line. Support for this hypothesis was provided by the interviews I conducted. One liberal Republican said:

> If I would have been ten years younger, I would have done what Riegle did (Don Riegle of Michigan switched from the Republican to the Democratic party). The Republican party I joined in the 1950s no longer operates. It started to change way back in 1964 with Goldwater, and it continued with Nixon and Reagan. That wing cost my good friend Jerry Ford the election in 1976, and, quite frankly, I don't like them. But today they are the party.

The flip side is provided by the following statement from a conservative Democrat:

> I did not belong in the same party as Ted Kennedy and Tip O'Neill. I didn't support them, and Lord knows Tip never did anything for me. Sure it made my decision to get out easier. Party is a source of strength for many members, but it was the source of a lot of headaches for me.

The lower an individual's party unity scores, the more likely that individual should be to retire, other things being equal.

Table 3-1 lists the variables described above, as well as the predicted sign of each variable's relationship with voluntary retirement. Tendency to retire should increase with age, seniority rank (the lower the rank, the higher the seniority), support for the conservative coalition, and identification as a southern Democrat or a Republican. Tendency to retire should decrease if the victory margin in the last election was high or if party unity scores are high.

Table 3-1

Predicted Relationship of Voluntary Retirement
and Seven Independent Variables

Variable	Predicted Sign
Age	+
Southern Democrat	+
Republican	+
Party Unity	-
Conservative Coalition	+
Seniority Rank	+
% Vote Received in Last Election	-

Where:

Dependent Variable = 1 if retire, 0 if not retire

Age = representative's age in years

Southern Democrat = 1 if Southern Democrat,
0 if not

Republican = 1 if Republican, 0 if not

Party Unity = party unity/(party opposition +
party unity) in the last year of
the Congress

Conservative Coalition = conservative coalition
support/(conservative coalition
opposition + support) in the last year
of the Congress

Seniority Rank = seniority rank in the relevant
Congress (1 = the highest rank
attainable)

% Vote Received in Last Election = % of the two-
party vote obtained by the representative in the last election

The Findings

When the variables in Table 3-1 are given the opportunity to discriminate between retirees and non-retirees in the ten Congresses from 1959 to 1978, the results presented in Table 3-2 are obtained. These figures represent the standardized canonical discriminant function coefficients of the variables. Since these coefficients are standardized, conclusions about the relative strengths of the variables can be made from the absolute values of the coefficients.

Age, not surprisingly, is the most powerful variable. Despite the emphasis on youthful retirements in many media treatments of the topic (see especially Abramson, 1980), we see that age, as predicted, is strongly and directly related to retirement during the period under study. Though it is the strongest variable, age is by no means the only variable of note. Both seniority rank and margin of victory in the last election are strongly related to voluntary retirement. The most surprising finding is that seniority is related to retirement in the opposite direction of that predicted. Other things being equal, as a member moves up the seniority ladder (i.e., as rank becomes lower), tendency to retire actually goes up. This finding would not be surprising except that age is controlled by virtue of its inclusion as a separate variable. More will be said about this finding in a later section.

Though the relationship between electoral safety and retirement (-.40) is consistent with our expectations, it is not consistent with the findings of past research. The earlier works all note that retirees tend to come from safe not marginal seats. This is certainly true, but there is an obvious reason. We have already seen that retirement is strongly related to age; and it is commonly known that percent of the two-party vote is positively related to age, that is, as a member moves through a career in the House, victory margins tend to increase (see Alford and Hibbing, 1981). Thus, it is not surprising that if the relationship between retirement and marginality is observed without controlling for age, it appears as though members who are electorally secure are the ones who are retiring (see Frantzich, 1978a:114-15; Cooper and West, 1981:85). By including both age and margin of victory in the discriminant function analysis, we see that, ceteris paribus, the greater the

Table 3-2

Standardized Canonical Discriminant
Function Coefficients,
1959-1978

Variable	Coefficient
Age	.72
Southern Democrat	.04
Republican	-.21
Party Unity	-.27
Conservative Coalition	.19
Seniority Rank	-.38
% Vote Received in Last Election	-.40

Where:
> the groups being discriminated between
> are retire (1) and not retire (0)

victory margin, the less likely the member is to retire voluntarily.

Three of the four remaining coefficients are also in the predicted direction. From 1959 to 1978, members with low party unity scores (mavericks) were indeed more likely to retire than those who strongly support their respective parties; conservatives were slightly more likely to retire than northern Democrats (the baseline group). This latter relationship is extremely weak as would be expected since the major reasons southern Democrats were expected to retire were their tendencies to deviate from the Democratic party line and to be conservative. Since these variables are included, little is left for the southern Democratic variable as an independent force.

The coefficient for Republicans is not in the expected direction, indicating that Republicans were actually less likely to retire than northern Democrats. It must be remembered that the influence of ideological frustration is controlled because of the inclusion of conservative coalition scores as a separate variable. The frustration resulting from being blocked from chairmanships apparently is an accepted part of life and is not a cause of retirement.

One potentially serious difficulty faced in drawing conclusions about the relative importance of the various independent variables stems from the fact that they may share a substantial amount of variance with each other. Though this multicollinearity would not alter conclusions about the ability of the overall model to discriminate between retirees and nonretirees, it could call into question statements about the strengths of individual variables. If two of the variables in Table 3-2 shared a high proportion of variance, we would not be able to place much confidence in their respective discriminant function coefficients. In order that determinations can be made regarding the extent to which multicollinearity is a problem, a correlation matrix which includes all of the independent variables employed in this study is presented in Table 3-3.

Given the nature of the independent variables, we would certainly expect a certain degree of collinearity. We know, for example, that whether or not the representative is a Republican is going to be related to conservative coalition support scores.

Table 3-3

Correlation Matrix

	Age	S.D.	Rep.	P.U.	C.C.	Sen.	Vote
Age	1.0						
Southern Democrat	.11	1.0					
Republican	-.04	-.39	1.0				
Party Unity	-.02	-.39	.03	1.0			
Conservative Coalition	.08	.25	.48	-.19	1.0		
Seniority	-.38	.07	-.43	.16	-.33	1.0	
% Vote in Last Election	.20	.46	-.32	-.21	.03	-.12	1.0

Thus the issue is whether these variables are so closely related that they cannot reasonable be thought of as distinct variables. The correlation coefficients in Table 3-3 reveal this is not the case. Though the correlations between some of the variables exceed .4, none rise to levels which would cause us to question the separate discriminating powers of the variables. In all instances in which the coefficients are over .4, one of the two dichotomous variables representing party affiliation is involved. Elsewhere (Hibbing, 1980) I attempt to sort out the role of party (and the variables correlated with it) in retirement decisions, but the important point here is that the level of multicollinearity is not severe enough to cause major alterations in conclusions about the relative strengths of the independent variables.

The Changing Nature of Voluntary Retirements

One issue which has not received the attention it deserves is the possibility that the causes of voluntary retirement have changed in recent years. The focus of previous research has tended to be on changes in the number of retirees even though an equally important change may have occurred in the reasons members voluntarily retire.

One way to find out whether there has been any change in the nature of voluntary retirements is to observe the changes in the ability of variables to discriminate between retirees and nonretirees. I have split the ten Congresses under study into two groups: the six Congresses before 1971, and the four Congresses after 1971. The reason for the uneven split is the relatively small number of retirees from the first six Congresses of the time period. The only way to obtain an approximately equal number of retirees in the "before" group and in the "after" group is to include fewer Congresses in the "after" group.[5] The procedures which resulted in Table 3-2 were then repeated on the members of the pre-1971 Congresses and on the members of the post-1971 Congresses. The results are presented in Table 3-4.

The changes in the standardized coefficients are quite informative and certainly supportive of the notion that the nature of voluntary retirements has changed. Perhaps the place to begin is to note that the predictions made in Table 3-1 are completely

Table 3-4

Standardized Canonical Discriminant
Function Coefficients,
Pre and Post 1971

Variable	Pre-1971 Coefficient	Post-1971 Coefficient
Age	.95	.45
Southern Democrat	.26	-.04
Republican	.10	-.39
Party Unity	-.27	-.19
Conservative Coalition	.05	.26
Seniority Rank	.03	-.70
% Vote Received in Last Election	-.50	-.29

Where:
the groups being discriminated between
are retire (1) and not retire (0)

accurate when the study is confined to the pre-1971 Congresses. Since problems arise in the post-1971 period, it is safe to conclude that the old way of thinking about voluntary retirements is no longer completely accurate. The motivations for retirement (and conversely the motivations to stay in the House) are not what they used to be.

The importance of age in explaining retirements has diminished markedly in the 1970s. In fact, it is no longer the strongest independent variable. The relative importance of age has been cut approximately in half. Other readily evident changes from the 1960s to the 1970s include the following: southern Democrats used to be more likely to retire than northern Democrats, but in the 1970s the relationship has reversed; Republicans used to be more likely to retire than northern Democrats, but now the relationship has reversed so that Republicans in the 1970s are _less_ likely to retire, other things being equal; the influence of deviation from the party line has weakened as has the importance of electoral insecurity; however the influence of a conservative ideology has increased.

But by far the largest change from the 1960s to the 1970s is the increase in the discriminating ability of seniority. From a very mildly positive relationship in the 1960s to an extremely strong negative relationship in the 1970s, the role of seniority in the decision to retire has been altered drastically. The direction of the relationship in the 1970s is not the direction which was expected. A fifty-year-old representative with a great deal of seniority should not be _more_ likely to retire than that same fifty-year-old with virtually no seniority, yet this is just what the sign of the relationship tells us. On the other hand, if we think carefully about some of the changes which occurred in the House in the early 1970s, the finding is not as illogical as it first seems -- in fact, it is not illogical at all.

As is obvious from the changes described in Chapter 1, seniority is no longer the only factor used in the process of selecting committee and sub-committee chairmen. Traits other than seniority have been considered in the 1970s. Though the demise of the seniority system has precipitated the removal of only three committee chairmen (all in 1975), it has had an extremely profound impact on the power structure of the House.

In addition to the three outright defeats of senior committee chairmen (W.R. Poage of Texas, F. Edward Hebert of Louisiana, and Wright Patman of Texas), there have been numerous close calls, starting in 1971 with John McMillan (D.-S.C.) of the District of Columbia Committee, and also several defeats of senior members in their bids to retain subcommittee chairs. The revival of the Democratic caucus may not have manifested itself in the deposition of numberous committee chairmen, but it has produced a fundamental shift in attitude. Senior chairmen can no longer feel completely secure since their behavior is not beyond reproach. Junior members now cast meaningful votes for or against these previously unassailable senior members. This situation has led many chairmen to resort to groveling before the junior members in efforts to convince the newcomers that they are not autocrats or demogagues. The significance of these changes is perhaps best illustrated by the following statement from a junior member of Congress who retired in 1978: "Before the reforms in the committee system, we were always expected to laugh at the jokes of the chairmen. After the reforms, it was amazing how funny our jokes became."

To those who have known what it is to be unquestioned committee bosses, a very painful adjustment was required, and apparently many preferred to retire from public life rather than make the adjustment. Thus, the fact that members with a large amount of seniority are retiring more than their ages (and other attributes) would predict is not surprising once the recent changes in the value of seniority are considered.[6]

The Recent Increase in Voluntary Retirements

As cautioned earlier, the major purpose of this chapter is to explain who retires, not to explain how many retire. However, since most people regard the increase in the number of retirements as the key research question, a brief look at some potential causes of the increase seems in order.

A multitude of explanations have been offered for the sudden increase in the number of voluntary retirements which took place in the 1970s. Some of these explanations include the so-called ethics provisions, the growing amount of time consumed by mundane constituency service work, a fractionalized legislative process, shrill constituents and abrasive single-issue interest groups, the disrespect and lack of privacy accorded politicians in this post-Watergate era, the large amount of fundraising required to conduct modern campaigns, self-centered and publicity conscious new members, improvements in the pension plan, lucrative private sector salaries, and the gradual aging of the membership, to name just a few. Since these reasons have been given substantial attention elsewhere (see Abramson, 1980; Buchanon, 1980; Cooper and West, 1981a and 1981b; Cover, 1981; Frantzich, 1978a and 1978b; Johnson, 1980; O'Brien, 1978; Rhodes, 1976; Sinclair, 1980), a thorough review of these diverse factors is not required here. For now suffice it to say many of the elements listed above contribute to what Cooper and West call an increased disaffection with congressional service, and certainly many have contributed to the increase in the number of voluntary retirements.

Yet another explanation is supplied by Albert Cover (1981). Cover views the increase as a movement back toward a systemic equilibrium subsequent to the disruptions caused by the extended congressional careers of the 1950s and 1960s. These extended careers resulted in a top-heavy age distribution and miniscule junior classes -- a situation conducive to a high retirement rate.

Support for Cover's notion is provided in Figure 3-1. The top graph in this figure presents the number of retirees by decade. Here the sharp drop between the 1950s and the 1960s is readily evident as is the even more extreme increase in the number of retirements between the 1960s and the 1970s. If, however, we aggregate the data by twenty year periods instead of ten, as is done in the lower graph, we see a much different pattern. The number of retirees in the last twenty years is virtually identical to the number of retirees in the 1940s and 1950s, and also in the 1920s and 1930s. Perhaps the 1970s merely counterbalanced the 1960s: a small number of retirements in the 1960s quite naturally led to a large number in the 1970s.

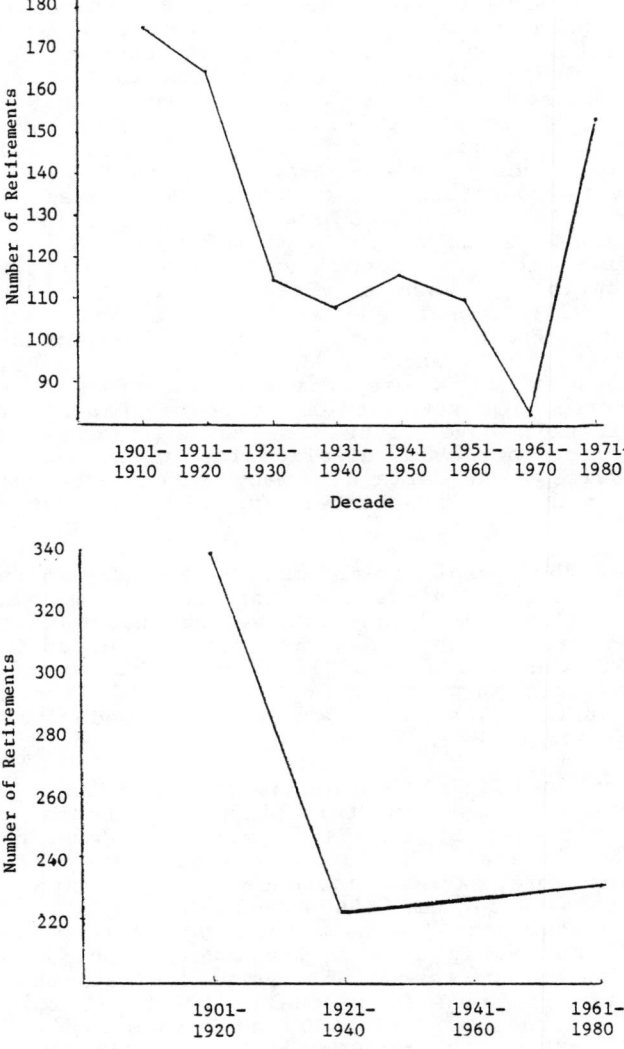

Figure 3-1.   Number of Voluntary Retirements Aggregated by Decade and by Twenty-Year
Periods.

92

This mechanical conception of voluntary retirement has merit, but it relies too heavily on age (tenure). The number of elderly members has some bearing on the number of retirees, but as we have already seen, many elderly members do not retire and many young members do. Members are not forced to retire after a certain number of terms of service. Just as the extended congressional career of the 1950s and 1960s was not an automatic response to the previous time period, the large number of retirements in the 1970s was not automatic. The glut of elderly members created the proper background for an increase in voluntary retirements, but this increase did not have to occur, and it did not have to occur in the 1970s. In addition, the earlier portions of this study showed that age is now less of a factor than it was in the 1960s, so an explanation based largely on the aging of the House due to extended careers is not entirely sufficient.

The explanation by Cover, as well as the explanation provided by Cooper and West is helpful, but many questions remain. I would like to suggest an explanation which has not been given much attention in previous research -- the demise of the seniority system.

Though the findings reported earlier in this chapter indicate that seniority clearly helps explain the changes in who retired in the 1970s, this does not necessarily mean seniority can help to explain the changes in the overall number who retired. A strong case can be made for why senior members should be disaffected by changes in the seniority system, but it seems as though the resultant increase in voluntary retirement in this group would be counterbalanced by a decrease in the number of junior members who voluntarily retire -- after all, these junior members now have the opportunity to move into crucial committee positions without waiting till they are in the twilight of their careers. This factor should lead to a decrease in the number of retirements by junior members, and the net result of changes in the seniority system on changes in the total number of retirees would be nill.

But this is not the case. Several factors combine to indicate that the effect of changes in the seniority system on the number of voluntary retirements has been far from nill. The first such factor is the comments of the retirees themselves. They argued forcefully that the reforms in the procedures used to select committee and subcommittee chairmen have had more to do with encouraging voluntary retirements than practically any other single factor. The members with a great deal of seniority were, quite naturally, the most vocal in their criticisms of these reforms. One former chairman told me:

> I was sickened by what they did to some of my friends. Some very outstanding chairmen were thrown out because a few punks were out for blood. I felt good about the strong support I received in the caucus, but how long would it have lasted? Most definitely these so-called reforms had something to do with my decision to leave.

But the senior members were not the only ones who claimed the seniority changes played a part in retirement decisions. The followinig two quotes came from middle-aged members of the 1978 retirement class:

> It used to be no one wanted to quit because they were always getting closer to the chairmanship. Today they figure "why wait around for fifteen years when it might not do any good?" The chair may not be given to you even if you have seniority. Besides, most members these days have as much power in their second term as they will in their eighth, so what is there to look forward to?

> In the old days, a member with 8 or 10 years of service was very reluctant to retire because he was throwing away years of stored capital, dues paying or whatever you want to call it. Now, 8 or 10 years means nothing. You're not giving up much by retiring because you might have been denied your chair even if you had the seniority. Why stay?

Even the very junior members recognized the encouragement to stay formerly offered by the seniority system. This statement was made by an individual who retired after serving only two terms:

I can see why careers used to be so
long. Members either had power or were
getting closer to it. Today, there are
no sure bets. Your power may go up or
down as you move through a career, or
you may be on a plateau for several
terms. The incentives for long careers
are not what they used to be.

The degree of increase in the number of voluntary retirements among different groups of representatives is also supportive of the seniority hypothesis.
If changes in the seniority rule are partially
responsible for the increase in voluntary retirements, we could reasonably expect the increase to be
most severe among those who are senior Democrats:
senior because these are the members who actually
lost power as a result of the reforms, and Democrats
because the attacks on the seniority system took[7]
place primarily within the Democratic caucus.
Increases in voluntary retirements among junior
members and among Republicans should not be as
severe, since changes in the seniority rule did not
hit them as hard.

The most careful group-by-group analysis of the
increase in voluntary retirements is that by Cooper
and West (1981a:88). Their figures do indeed
indicate that, though retirements are up (from the
1960s to the 1970s) in every category of member, the
sharpest increase is within the group composed of
Democrats who were committee or subcommittee chairmen. A quick look at the seniority ranks of the
retiring members also illustrates this point. In
1968, for example, the seniority ranks of retiring
Democrats were 7, 10, 18, 22, 24, 32, 33, 51, and 67.
But in 1978 the seniority ranks of some of the retiring Democrats were 1, 2, 4, 6, 7, 8, 10, 12, 14, 15,
and 18. Clearly, some very high ranking Democrats
were leaving in 1978, and 1978 was not atypical for
the post-reform years; the mean rank of retiring
Democrats before 1971 was nearly 40, while after 1971
the mean dropped to 24.

The number of "junior" members who are retiring
is up, but not by a large margin. And as is evident
from Table 3-4, though in the 1960s Republicans were
more likely to retire than northern Democrats, in the
1970s they became less likely to retire, other things
being equal. Obviously Republicans are not the group
responsible for the large increase in the number of

voluntary retirments.[8] The fact that senior Democrats make up the group for which the retirement rate increased most sharply supports the seniority hypothesis, and the fact that there has been some increase among the other groups does nothing to harm the hypothesis since there has been a decrease for all members in the value of a long career.

Finally, the timing of the increase is perfectly consistent with the appearance of the first chinks in the armor of seniority. In 1971 when the 92nd Congress was being organized the Democratic caucus let it be known that seniority need not be considered by the committee on committees (then the members of the Ways and Means Committee), members were given the opportunity to request a secret ballot on individual chairmen, and these tools were shown to be more than cosmetic changes as the caucus did vote and record many negative ballots. The increase in voluntary retirements ensued at the end of this same 92nd Congress and has remained at a high level since. So, unlike many other explanations, the seniority hypothesis is able to explain the precise timing of the increase in retirements.

While it would be foolish to claim there is only one reason for the increase in the number of voluntary retirements, the evidence strongly suggests the demise of the seniority rule to be an important contributing factor.

Conclusion

The research presented here has several implications for the congressional system and for our understanding of its operation. These implications will be discussed in the final chapter of this study, but three merit brief mention here. The first concerns the nature of recent membership turnover in the House. Though in the 1970s voluntary retirement and not electoral defeat was the major source of membership turnover, the immediate impact of voluntary retirement on public policy outcomes is discounted by both Frantzich (1978a:123-25) and Cooper and West (1981a:92) because the scores of retirees on roll call scales of liberal/conservative voting tend to be similar to the scores of their successors. The research presented here indicates that if the focus is broadened beyond roll call voting the impact of voluntary retirement on public policy may not be all that minimal. One of the key findings of this study is that the type of individual who tends to retire changed appreciably between the 1960s and the 1970s. Whereas in the 1960s retirees tended to be those who were not in the dominant group (i.e., retirees tended to be Republicans or southern Democrats who were electorally insecure and lacking in seniority), in the 1970s massive increases took place in the proportional retirement rate within the supposedly dominant group -- Democrats with a good deal of seniority (many of them committee or subcommittee chairmen). With key people leaving, it is reasonable to suppose that the impact of voluntary retirement on the functioning and general policy-making of the House was much greater in the 1970s than in previous decades.

Though the policy impact of voluntary retirement may be greater than was previously supposed, the main value of studying voluntary retirement still eminates from the role it can play in answering questions about the status of the House and the motivations of its members. For example, Charles O. Jones asks the question, "Will Reform Change Congress?" (1977), and proceeds to fit the reforms of the 1970s into the larger stream of congressional change, thereby permitting a better base from which to look at the Congress of the future. In two ways my research speaks to the issues which concern Jones. First, the reforms may have changed the House in a somewhat unexpected way -- by changing the membership of the body. While the question of whether or not the reforms will result in better public policy is virtually impossible to answer, we can say with some degree of certainty that a partial consequence of the reforms is that this policy is being made by less experienced legislators. Second, questions are raised about the overall pattern of change in the House. The extended congressional careers which resulted from the "profitable and professional" House of the 1950s and 1960s (Bullock, 1972:1295) were thought to be an integral feature of the institutionalized House. What then are we to conclude when the average career suddenly becomes much shorter and the voluntary retirement rate soars? Either the House has ceased its march toward institutionalization or the concept of institutionalization as it has been applied to legislatures needs to be reconsidered.

A final implication involves the forces which motivate members of Congress -- a topic which has been the focus of a good deal of attention. David

Mayhew (1974) makes a strong case for the belief that the sole motivation of members of Congress is the desire to be re-elected. More recently, some scholars have contended that congressmen want to do more than get back in; they want to maximize their power within the body (see, for example, Jones and Woll, 1979; and Dodd, 1977). The findings presented here support the latter view. Representatives are motivated by the desire to acquire committee power. When the seniority rule was an iron law, the way to maximize power was to stay in the House for an extended career. When the application of the seniority rule became a question mark, the value of an extended congressional career declined. As a result, the voluntary retirement rate shot up and the typical congressional career was shortened. Though the desire to be re-elected certainly weighs heavily on the minds of representatives (in fact, power in the House cannot be maximized if one is not re-elected to the House), it appears as though an emphasis on this motivation to the exclusion of all others would give a less than accurate portrayal of congressional motivations. Indeed, the very existence of a high retirement rate goes against the belief that every member of Congress wants, above all else, to be re-elected.

Footnotes

[1] This particular time period was selected so that there would be a substantial number of cases both before and after the 1972 increase in the number of voluntary retirements.

[2] Since conservative coalition support scores are lowered by failure to vote, I have corrected the support scores by dividing the support score by the sum of the support score and the opposition score. Thus, if a member had a conservative coalition support score of 40 and an opposition score of 20, the attendance-corrected score used in this study would be 67. A similar correction procedure was applied to the party unity scores.

[3] Another measure of electoral insecurity was tested. This variable is the change in the percent of the two-party vote received by the member in his election four years ago to the percent received in the last election. The idea behind this variable is that a narrow victory margin may not be as good an indicator of electoral insecurity as a declining victory margin. However, this variable did not perform as well as the simple mean share of the two-party vote in the last election. (In addition, the number of cases was substantially reduced since all members who failed to serve at least two consecutive terms had to be removed.) Consequently, this variable is not included in the analysis.

[4] It should be noted that a variant of the electoral insecurities hypothesis is the notion that an impending redistricting will influence a member to retire voluntarily (see Frantzich, 1978a; and Cooper and West, 1981). My analysis revealed that voluntary retirements in 1962 and 1972 did tend to come in disproportionately high numbers from states that redistricted. These years witnessed alterations in many district lines as a result of the decennial census. On the other hand, in 1966 and 1968 -- two years with high levels of redistricting due to the Supreme Court's reapportionment decisions -- voluntary retirements did <u>not</u> tend to occur in the states that redistricted. Apparently retirements were influenced by redistricting only when the more severe disruptions associated with the census-based redistricting (no states gained or lost seats in 1966 or 1968) took place. Since the exclusion of 1966 and

1968 leaves only two relevant years in the study, the redistricting variable is not employed in the multivariate analysis (see Hibbing, 1980:89-92, for a thorough discussion of the redistricting variable).

[5]In addition, manipulation of the breakpoint revealed that the point selected produced the biggest discrepancy between coefficients for the pre and post groups. The change in the causes of voluntary retirement seems to have occurred in the early 1970s.

[6]The emphasis placed on the role of seniority leads us, once again, to question its status as a distinct variable. Specifically, if seniority is highly correlated with age, the separate explanatory power of age and seniority could not be properly assessed. Certainly we would expect some relationship, but as Table 3-3 reveals, age and seniority are correlated at only .38. The widely varying ages at which members enter the House (one of the individuals I interviewed was nearly 60 when he first entered the House) and the separate seniority rankings for Democrats and Republicans are two important factors which lower this correlation. Since nearly two-thirds of the variance of each of these variables is not shared with the other, our treatment of the variables as separate entities is not jeopardized.

[7]Another reason for this expectation is that ranking minority memberships may not be desired to the extent that they structure behavior the way committee chairmanships seem to.

[8]A look at the data shows that Republicans were indeed not as affected by the seniority changes. When the procedures which produced the post-1971 findings of Table 3-4 are performed separately for the Democrats and Republicans, the coefficient for seniority is -.29 for the Republicans and -.89 for the Democrats. As expected, the strength of the overall relationship derives largely from the Democrats.

CHAPTER 4

THE CONSEQUENCES OF VOLUNTARY RETIREMENT

Till now, I have attempted to determine the causes of voluntary retirement from the U.S. House. In this chapter the focus shifts to the consequences of the decision to leave. Does retirement matter to the political system? Has the recent increase in retirement caused any change in Congress; if so, what?

Turnover

An obvious consequence of voluntary retirements is membership turnover. Retiring members leave, thereby making room for newcomers. In this respect, voluntary retirements are no different than electoral defeats, deaths in office, or resignations. All these events lead to the replacement of one representative with another. But this is not an analysis of congressional turnover in general; such efforts have been undertaken elsewhere (see Huntington, 1965; and Jewell and Patterson, 1977, for good general discussions of turnover in legislative bodies). My interest is in whether or not voluntary retirement is a distinct form of turnover. If voluntary retirement does indeed create a different kind of turnover than, say, electoral defeat or death in office, the consequences could be quite important due to the shifts in the source of congressional turnover which have occurred in recent decades.

Contrary to popular belief, turnover levels in the House have not changed much in the last thirty years. The total number of House newcomers in the 1970s was up very slightly from both the totals for the 1960s and the 1950s (see Table 4-1). Turnover in the 1970s was not abysmally low, and the level of turnover was not much different than the level of turnover in the two previous decades. What did change greatly in the 1970s was the composition or sources of this turnover. As Table 4-1 shows, the percentage of membership turnover attributable to voluntary retirement was higher in the 1970s than at any other time in this century. Conversely, the percentage of membership turnover attributable to electoral defeat (in both primary and general elections) is lower than at any other time in this

Table 4-1

Relative Importance of the Sources
of House Turnover, By Decades

Decade	% From Electoral Defeats	% From Voluntary Retirements	% From Other Sources	Total Turnover (N)	
1901-10	40.5	34.2	22.3	100%	(511)
1911-20	43.9	29.8	26.3	100%	(551)
1921-30	45.8	25.4	28.8	100%	(448)
1931-40	54.0	18.4	27.6	100%	(587)
1941-50	51.4	23.7	24.9	100%	(490)
1951-60	39.8	31.8	28.4	100%	(349)
1961-70	45.5	23.3	31.2	100%	(347)
1971-80	35.3	38.1	26.6	100%	(402)

century. The third category listed in Table 4-1 consists primarily of deaths in office and retirements to try for other public offices. This category has remained essentially stable throughout the century. The trade-off in the 1970s was between voluntary retirements and electoral defeats. During that decade, not even one out of three new members secured seats by defeating incumbents. There has been an unmistakable shift in the relative importance of the sources of turnover, so that voluntary retirement now is the major source of turnover in the House. Relying on aggregate turnover figures masks important changes in congressional turnover.

But if voluntary retirement has the same consequences as electoral defeat, the shift in the source of turnover makes no difference. Does it matter that voluntary retirement is now the major source of congressional turnover, or do all kinds of turnover have the same consequences?

A partial answer to this question can be found in past research. Stephen Frantzich hypothesizes that retirees will often be replaced by people of similar partisan and ideological persuasions. The reasoning is simple: the fact that the retiring member is leaving is not necessarily due to a repudiation by the voters of his/her beliefs and efforts while in Congress but is due to a voluntary decision by the member to leave the House. This is quite unlike the situation of a member who leaves because of electoral defeat. Presumably, the voters removed this member from office because they wanted somebody new and different. Consequently, newcomers who replace defeated members could be expected to differ in some significant way from their predecessors while newcomers who replace retirees may be quite similar to the retirees -- perhaps they were even members of the retirees' staffs.

This hypothesis is clearly supported if the focus is on the partisanship of the predecessor and successor. From the 89th Congress to the 95th there were 350 departures due either to voluntary retirement or electoral defeat. Twenty-six of these cases are not suitable for this analysis as a result of a member failing to serve a complete term or being victimized by an extended illness. I gathered information on the predecessors and successors in each of the remaining 324 cases of membership turnover. Table 4-2 displays findings which bear on the party switch hypothesis. It shows that when turnover is caused by voluntary retirements the successor is likely to be of the same party as the predecessor. When electoral defeat is the source of turnover, the successor, not surprisingly, is usually a member of the other major party. In 71.7 percent of the cases of voluntary retirement from these seven Congresses, the successor has been a member of the same party as the retiree. In contrast, in only 20.7 percent of the cases of electoral defeat was the successor a member of the same party as the defeated member. The source of turnover makes a major difference in the likelihood of a membership switch entailing a party switch.

Table 4-2

Percentage of Turnover Resulting in Party
Switches By Source of Turnover --
89th to 95th Congresses

	Voluntary Retirements	Electoral Defeats
% Same Party	71.7% (104)	20.7% (37)
% Party Switch	28.3% (41)	79.3% (142)
Total	100% (145)	100% (179)

tau b = .51; lambda = .45

When the emphasis is shifted to the ideological match of predecessor and successor, the work of Frantzich is relevant. He finds:

...that in over half of the cases involving static ambition (electoral defeats) successors were in the oppo- site half of the House compared to their predecessors. In the discrete and progressive ambition cases (volun- tary retirement and retirement to run for higher office) this situation happened in approximately 30 percent of the cases (1978a:124).

Frantzich's methodology is open to question on one point. He tests the hypothesis by first determin- ing the mean roll call score of members on a liberal- ism index. He then recorded whether the departing members were above or below this mean. Likewise, he determined whether the newcomers were above or below the mean for their first Congress. Change, according to Frantzich, only occurs when the departing member is on one side of the mean and the successor is on the other. In other words, if we assume the mean liberalism score in two successive Congresses is 50, a departing member who scored 49 would be classified as "unlike" the successor if this newcomer scored 51. Conversely, a retiree who scored 0 would be "like" a successor who scored 49. By classifying people into one of only two categories, Frantzich has lost a lot of information, and his findings may even be distor- ted.

A preferable procedure is to average the total amount of change in ideological position resulting from electoral defeat, and to do the same for volun- tary retirement. I have made these calculations for the seven-Congress period described earlier. I used the ratings provided by the Americans for Constitu- tional Action (ACA) to represent the members' positions on the ideological spectrum. The results are presented in Table 4-3.

Obviously, the source of turnover makes a differ- ence in the relationship of the roll call (ACA) scores of successor and predecessor. Table 4-3 reveals that, as hypothesized, the differences are greater when the turnover is caused by electoral defeat than when it is caused by voluntary retire- ment. The mean absolute value of the change in ACA scores from the retires' scores in the first term of their last Congress to the newcomers' scores in the first term of their first Congress is 21.71 points. When the source of turnover is electoral defeat, the

Table 4-3

Mean Absolute Change in ACA Scores by Source
of Turnover -- 89th to 95th Congress

Source	Mean Change in ACA Scores (N)
Electoral Defeat	47.36 (179)
Voluntary Retirement	21.71 (145)

F = 91.62; significance level = .001

same calculation yields a mean change of 47.36 --
over twice as large a change in scores. Thus, though
I believe the procedures used here are more appropriate, the findings are quite consistent with those of
Professor Frantzich.

One final issue relating to successor-
predecessor relations deserves mention. Naturally, a
switch in party generally brings with it a large
shift in liberalism/conservatism scores. Is the
smaller shift in ideological scores due entirely to
the smaller number of party switches which result
when voluntary retirement is the source of turnover?
It is not difficult to determine whether or not the
entire difference in degree of change in ACA scores
is attributable to the disproportionate number of
party switches associated with electoral defeats. In
Tables 4-4 and 4-5, turnover has been split into two
groups: that which entailed a party switch and that
which did not. Once this split is made, the biasing
effects described above are removed, and the procedure used to obtain Table 4-3 can be duplicated.

Table 4-4 shows that even when we concentrate on
only those districts in which the new representatives
were of a different party than the old representatives, electoral defeat spurs a bigger change in ACA
scores (from former members to new members) than does
voluntary retirement. (The number of cases reflects
what we found earlier -- that most cases involving
party switches are related to electoral defeats.)

Table 4-4

Mean Absolute Change in ACA Scores When Turnover
Involved a Party Switch--89th to 95th Congresses

Turnover Source	Mean Change in ACA Scores (N)
Electoral Defeat	55.30 (142)
Voluntary Retirement	38.05 (41)

F = 17.96; significance level = .001

Table 4-5

Mean Absolute Change in ACA Scores When
Turnover Did Not Entail a Party Switch--
89th to 95th Congresses

Turnover Source	Mean Change in ACA Scores (N)
Electoral Defeat	17.70 (37)
Voluntary Retirement	15.27 (104)

F = .67; significance level = .41

Table 4-5, on the other hand, is limited to cases in which turnover did <u>not</u> involve a switch in the party of the district's representative. (This time the "N" for voluntary retirements is the one that suffers.) Again we see that electoral defeat generally causes a type of turnover in which successor is more unlike predecessor, although in this instance the difference is not statistically significant.

Changes in Behavior Prior to Departure

A great deal of the importance of ambition theory lies in its ability to connect ambition to behavior. Knowledge of the nature and causes of ambition among politicians would lose much of its significance if variations in behavior were not tied to variations in ambition. Yet, this is precisely the situation in which we find ambition theory.

Even though Joseph Schlesinger states that "the central assumption of ambition theory is that a politician's behavior is a response to his office goals" (1966:6), he spends virtually no time addressing this matter, choosing instead to concentrate on the "opportunity structure" of public offices. Unfortunately, most subsequent research has followed Schlesinger's lead in stressing the factors that influence ambition (Frost, 1972; Black, 1972; Mezey, 1970; Fishel, 1971 and 1973; Kritzer, 1978; Rohde, 1979).

Indicators of ambition have been considered frequently as dependent variables but very sparingly as independent variables. Most of the time, <u>behavior</u> has been used to explain <u>ambition</u> (if a representative runs for the Senate, he must have progressive ambition) rather than <u>ambition</u> being used to explain <u>behavior</u> (if a representative aspires to the Senate, he will alter his voting pattern in order to appeal to the broader constituency).

This emphasis is not misplaced. Many of these studies, for example, contribute to our knowledge of the kind of politician who is likely to run for higher office. The initial chapters of this analysis address the question of the kinds of representatives who are most likely to retire. In a variety of ways, analyzing such questions is important and informative. But it is just as important to investigate ambition as a cause rather than an effect.

The importance of ambition as a phenomenon to be explained is evident if we visualize a representative democracy in which politicians have no desire to get re-elected. If elections are to have any chance of serving as a means by which the people exert some control over public officials, ambition on the part of these officials is prerequisite. As Schlesinger states:

> A political system unable to kindle ambition for office is as much in danger of breaking down as one unable to restrain ambitions. Representative government, above all, depends on a supply of men so driven; the desire for election and, more important, for re-election becomes the electorate's restraint upon its public officials. No more irresponsible government is imaginable than one of highminded men unconcerned for their political fortunes (1966:2).

It is hardly arguable that if public officials have no desire for re-election, the public will be hard pressed to affect the behavior of these officials.

Recently there has been some dispute over whether or not the desire for re-election (static ambition) is beneficial to the system. Several political scientists have suggested that this desire is deleterious. David Mayhew's Congress: The Electoral Connection (1974) is one example. Mayhew makes the assumption that every member of Congress is motivated solely by the desire for re-election. He procedes to show that much of what goes on in and around Congress can be explained with this assumption. In Mayhew's skillful hands, all the pieces seem to fit, but the resulting picture is far from flattering. Representatives are shown to be more concerned with posturing than with making good legislation. They advertise themselves with all kinds of mailings, they take positions they hope will get a lot of play back home, and they scheme to get into positions which will allow them to take credit for various actions. In all, the quality of legislation is not of prime concern.

Edward Tufte (1978) also questions the consequences of the electoral connection. Tufte details the avalanche of benefits which congressmen and the president unleash on constituents prior to an election. Members of Congress to some extent and presidents to a great extent are said to hedge their bets in election years by instituting tax cuts and by pouring forth additional benefits of all kinds on the public. It is thought that this generosity will help put the people in the "correct" frame of mind for the election. Though voters do not seem to object to this largesse, it will be disasterous in the long run. This behavior creates, says Tufte, "a lurching, stop-and-go economy...There is a bias toward policies with immediate, highly visible benefits and deferred, hidden costs -- myopic policies for myopic voters" (1978:143). Again, the conclusion is that the personal ambitions of public officials influence behavior but not in a manner beneficial to the long-term interests of the country.

Along similar lines, Morris Fiorina (1977) speculates that members of Congress, because of their desire to secure re-election, deliberately enlarge the bureaucracy for electoral benefit. They do this because the larger the bureaucracy, the more likely it is that constituents will need help in dealing with various aspects of that bureaucracy. If constituents ask their representatives for assistance and representatives cheerfully render it, then constituents will more likely vote for the representatives who "took on" the bureaucracy for them. Once again, the desire for re-election has manifested itself in a behavior that is good for public officials in the short-term but bad for the country in the long-term.

In addition to these criticisms of the desire for re-election, the media seem anxious to trace almost any occurrence to the re-election motivations of politicians. The interpretation presented by the media often involves a politician blatantly attempting to secure votes and giving no consideration to other potential consequences. It is little wonder there has been talk of down-playing the role of elections in democratic countries like our own, given the emphasis of the mass media on the alleged self-serving performance of politicians -- leaking classified weapons information, prolonging life-endangering events, mindlessly expanding the bureaucracy, or spending the social security program into bankruptcy for the purpose, so it is claimed, only of getting re-elected.

Limitation of the number of permissible terms of service is the reform most frequently advocated to check the self-serving tendencies of elected politicians. After only a short time in office, Jimmy Carter stated that he favored a six-year, non-renewable presidential term, saying that his every move was assumed to be the product of personal ambition rather than a desire to do what was best for the country. Others have advocated a limit on the number$_1$ of terms senators and representatives could serve.[1] Regardless of the office involved, a mandatory term limit would remove the sanction of the vote for large portions of the period of service (and, in the case of the Carter proposal, for the entire period of service). An official who knows that his present term must, by law, be his last is immune from the sanction of the vote. There can be no threat of voting that official out of office.

Certainly there are many who oppose changes of this kind and who defend the right of the people to sanction public officials through the vote. Most observers give the proposals to limit terms very little chance of passing in the near future. But the debates on this topic can be very heated. The two sides embrace completely different philosophies of the proper role of the electorate in government. These differing philosophies are evident in the two quotes that follow. Both were taken from the same section of the same Sunday newspaper:

> He (Jimmy Carter) must divide his time between campaigning and governing, and he seems incapable of guiding the country and running for president simultaneously. Indeed, he is so bent on re-election that he is letting politics influence his policies. That, of course, is nothing new among sitting presidents. But, given the state of the world today, it is tragic (<u>Des Moines Register</u>, 1980).

> In a second term, unrestrained by not having to face the electorate again, and seeking to make up for the miserable period behind us, Carter

might run off in dangerous directions (Rowen, 1980).

Though these statements were printed virtually side-by-side, they represent philosophies that are poles apart. In the first, we are told that it is "tragic" for an elected official to let politics (a desire for re-election) interfere with policies, while in the second we are told that, if that same official does not have to worry about re-election, he "might run off in dangerous directions." What are we to do?

The first thing we should do is determine the actual impact of the electoral connection. Normative theorizing about the role of ambition needs to be based on an undestanding of the role ambition <u>does</u> play. Only by determining the exact role of the desire for re-election will we be able to make accurate claims about required changes in the system.

Unfortunately, this is an area where systematic research is lacking. To be sure, this topic has not been completely ignored by researchers. The three essays already mentioned -- those by Mayhew, Tufte, and Fiorina -- have much to say about the manner in which political behavior is influenced by the desire for re-election. But Mayhew and Fiorina provide no evidence beyond two case studies, numerous anecdotes, and some persuasive prose. Tufte includes some evidence, but it is not exactly evidence pertaining to personal ambition. Tufte found that presidents made some attempt to influence the outcome of elections even when the presidents themselves were not running for re-election. Thus, it is not entirely correct to treat Tufte's work as a statement of the role of <u>personal</u> ambition in the behavior of public officials. The ambition described is often oriented more toward some collectivity (party) than toward the individual.

In addition to these studies, others have relevance to the topic of the role of ambition in the behavior of office-holders. James David Barber (1965) discusses the different behavior which can be expected of public officials given their reasons for seeking office in the first place. Barber, studying Connecticut state legislators, discovered a wide variance in behavior (participation in floor debates, writing legislation, and generally being a more or less active legislator). He makes a persuasive case for the view that an important part of the explanation for variations in legislators behavior lies in their different goals or ambitions.

Kenneth Prewitt and William Nowlin (1969) claim to uncover some behavioral consequences of ambition. Certainly the title of their article, "Political Ambitions and the Behavior of Incumbent Politicians," implies that they tie ambition firmly to behavior. But Prewitt and Nowlin have nothing to say about the behavior of incumbent politicians. Their only concern is with the responses of Bay Area city councilmen to a set of questions. Though they find that answers to these questions vary with the ambitions possessed by the councilmen, the connection between responses to survey questions and actual behavior is not attempted.

Barbara Deckard (1972) may have found some consequences of the ambitions of members of the U.S. House of Representatives. Her focus of concern is somewhat limited (her tentative finding is that if there are too many members of a state delegation who want to move on to other offices, the delegation will tend not to be very cohesive), but at least this is an attempt to connect ambitions (office goals) to actual behavior.

Finally, Stephen Frantzich (1978a and 1978b) has briefly addressed the effects of ambition. Frantzich hypothesizes, much as we will shortly, that since the decision to retire constitutes a change from static to discrete ambition, a behavioral change should accompany this change in ambition. Frantzich tests this hypothesis in a less than satisfactory manner, but his research does represent an effort to analyze the crucial link between ambition and behavior in elected officials.

Thus, though the topic has not received the attention it deserves, neither has it been ignored. In the remainder of this chapter, I will refine and extend past efforts to specify the role of ambition in American politics in general, and in the House of Representatives in particular.

The Study

All of this may seem a far cry from the consequences of voluntary retirements, but it is not. One of the problems facing research on ambitions has been the presumed lack of variance in political ambition.

Many believe with Mayhew that every member of Congress wants to get re-elected more than anything else. Others agree with Rohde (1979) that <u>all</u> politicians want to move up to a better office. Seldom has there been recognition of the fact that many want to get out. There was little disagreement when Frank Kent wrote that leaving political office "is never in the least voluntary...Every man who has held elective office wants to keep it or get a better one" (1936:177). Stephen Frantzich notes that if one spends very long reviewing the literature:

> Without too much urging, we begin to believe that the only way incumbent politicians leave office is in a pine box, or in a few cases kicking and screaming on the heels of electoral defeat (1978b:2).

As we have seen in earlier chapters, such beliefs simply are not true. Many incumbent politicians including many incumbent members of Congress do <u>not</u> want to stay in office.

When a sizable group of members retire from the House, researchers are provided with a basis for comparison. Those who seek re-election to the House constitute a control group, since their ambitions can be considered static. This control group can be compared to the group of members whose ambitions have changed, reflected by their decision to retire. The political strategies which congressmen think are necessary to re-election success can be unmasked by determining how retiring members change their behavior once electoral constraints have been removed. This test will indicate the degree to which representatives are willing to allow their personal desires to be modified by external factors -- factors that are thought to be valuable for re-election purposes. By observing what happens when these ambitions are removed, we can assess the degree to which they influence behavior when present.[2]

Such a test will be conducted by assuming that the decision to retire is made several months before the end of the term. My interviews with retirees indicate that this assumption is realistic -- nearly all 1978 retirees had firm plans to retire by late in 1977, months before the end of the 95th Congress.

Additional evidence indicates that the 1978 retiring class is not unusual in this regard. Around February, _Congressional Quarterly Weekly Report_ lists those members who have announced their retirements. This list always includes the lion's share of all those who eventually decide to retire at the end of the relevant Congress, and those who have announced certainly do not constitute all those who have _decided_ to get out of public service (several retirees told me that they made the decision long before they announced it). Accordingly, it is utterly reasonable to assume that retiring representatives are aware in their last year in office that they will not be participating in the upcoming election. In effect, the change from static to discrete ambition has disconnected the electoral connection. This uncoupling should result in behavioral changes between the first year of the last Congress and the last year of that Congress (what will be the last year of House service). Those running for re-election should exhibit milder behavioral changes, since their ambition (as judged by office-seeking behavior) has remained the same.

To measure the behavioral changes of representatives from the first year of a Congress to the second, the scores of individual representatives on various roll call voting scales have been recorded: participation scores, presidential support scores, party unity scores, conservative coalition support scores, and Americans for Constitutional Action scores have all been recorded for each year of the last ten Congresses. Our dependent variable is the _change_ in a representative's voting scores from one year to the next. The basic hypothesis is that those who retire (change ambitions) will exhibit greater changes in voting scores than will those who seek re-election to the same House seat. It will not matter to the analysis if the content of the voting scales is not strictly comparable from one year to the next, since we are comparing changes. The analysis concerns differences between retirees and non-retirees, and not differences in members' individual scale scores which may reflect changes in substantive content.

Such a study design cannot resolve all problems. The data came entirely from roll call votes. Though voting in the House is a vital part of a represntative's job, it is by no means the only part. A representative may remain consistent in roll call behavior after the decision to retire, but change his other behavior substantially. He may quit going back to the district, he may go back more often than ever, he may change his "home style" when he is in the district, or he may change his relations with the staff, attendance and contributions to committee sessions, or the number of junkets taken. None of these changes would be tapped by the measures of behavior we are using here, and there is a good possibility many of these changes do occur. Several of the retirees I spoke with mentioned changes in these areas:

> Sure I took more trips. _____ and I sort of had a contest going to see who could do the most traveling. We let word get around that we were available to replace anybody who could not go on a trip for one reason or another. I filled several of these vacancies because many members were too busy running for re-election to take the trips they had set up.

> I suppose I goofed off a little. I don't feel guilty about it because things slowed way down at the office. Lobbyists pretty much forget about you once you announce, my staff was busy trying to hook on with some other member, constituents think you leave office as soon as you announce, so there was not a lot to do.

> My trips back to the district went way down. There was no reason to go back. My engagement calendar used to be booked up for seven or eight months in advance; after I announced, no one seemed anxious for me to be at their graduation or on their radio talk show. I stayed in town and found out that Washington was not as bad as I had thought all those years.

Insofar as comparing the behavior of retirees to non-retirees is a useful way of understanding the role of ambition in politics, future studies will want to make this comparison on the basis of forms of behavior unrelated to roll call voting.

Another problem with this research design is that to the extent retirement decisions are not made precisely between the two halves of a Congress, we have a conservative test of the hypothesis. For example, if a decision to retire is made immediately after the last election, we would not expect a great deal of behavioral change between the first and last sessions of the ensuing Congress, since in both years the representative knew he would not be running for re-election. Unfortunately, given the bluntness of the roll call data, this problem cannot be solved.

Finally, it is likely I have overstated the case in describing the basis for this research. There is no reason to expect that a retirement decision will create a completely new representative in the waning months of his service. Not all constraints on the member's behavior are removed; only electoral constraints. Important social constraints probably remain. For example, a member may not want to alienate trusted friends and allies (both on and off the Hill) by a sudden reversal of positions. Nonetheless, given the importance usually attached to electoral constraints, we can still reasonably expect observable behavioral changes subsequent to the retirement decision.

A further point needs to be made before we turn to the findings. Two groups of representatives have been removed from the analysis: those who ran for other elective office, and those who did not serve a complete term because of death, severe illness, late entry, or some other reason. Those who run for other office are excluded because I am seeking to compare those whose ambition changed with those whose ambition did not change. Those who decided to run for other office have new ambitions and therefore cannot be included with those seeking re-election to the House. Neither can they be included with retirees, since changing the electoral connection may have consequences different from disconnecting it completely. The issue of the behavioral consequences of a change in ambition which results in a desire to please a new constituency is left for another study. Here we keep within the theme of this study by concentrating on those whose ambitions are changing from static to discrete; that is, those who are voluntarily retiring and not seeking other elective office. The second group excluded here -- those who did not serve the complete Congress -- is removed because we need the scores from both years of each Congress to make the desired comparisons. Cases must be removed if figures are not available for both years.

Roll Call Participation

The first type of roll call behavior we will analyze is <u>simple participation</u>; that is, the percentage of the recorded votes on which the representative voted yea or nay. The hypothesis is that those who choose not to run for re-election can afford to allow their attendance to drop after their decisions are made. Those who are running for re-election will want to keep participation levels high, since no member wants to give an opponent the opportunity to make an election issue out of a spotty attendance record. Table 4-6 presents the mean change in participation scores for retirees and non-retirees for the ten elections under study.

As can be seen, attendance in the election or second year of Congresses is almost invariably down for all groups, but our interest is in comparing the mean attendance drop of retirees to that registered by non-retirees. Here, as expected, we see that the drop for retirees is greater. In every Congress examined in this study, the participation of retirees drops more sharply than the participation of those who ran for re-election.[3] The mean drop of retirees in these ten Congresses is 7.53 greater than the mean drop registered by non-retirees in these same Congresses.

The fact that participation goes down greatly subsequent to retirement decisions is not surprising if we think back to some of the comments of the members of the 1978 retirement class (see Chapter 3). Many of them were very irritated by the number of roll call votes in the House. Once the need to keep a good attendance record is no longer present, members act to remove this irritant by missing some of the recorded votes. If the electoral connection does nothing else, we can be quite sure that it encourages a good attendance record.

Presidential Support Scores

Another roll call rating score compiled by Congressional Quarterly is the percentage of some selected votes on which the representative voted in agreement with the president's position.[4] Here expectations are somewhat more uncertain than with

Table 4-6

Mean Changes in Participation Levels From
First to Second Years of Ten Recent Congresses

Congress (Years)	Non-retirees (N of Cases)		Retirees (N of Cases)	
86th (1959-60)	- .69	(409)	- 5.32	(19)
87th (1961-62)	-4.13	(407)	-23.50	(18)
88th (1963-64)	.03	(406)	- 9.86	(22)
89th (1965-66)	-8.57	(411)	-13.24	(17)
90th (1967-68)	-3.63	(413)	-12.23	(13)
91st (1969-70)	-5.28	(407)	- 5.38	(8)
92nd (1971-72)	-1.55	(396)	-10.17	(30)
93rd (1973-74)	-1.70	(392)	- 7.76	(29)
94th (1975-76)	-2.04	(388)	-10.00	(26)
95th (1977-78)	-1.70	(386)	- 7.06	(31)

t = 4.05; difference in means = -7.53

regard to participation scores. When a representative is released from the sanction of the vote, would we expect support of the president to go up or down? The answer depends upon the situation; the popularity of the president, the party identification of the president and the representative, and personal factors all come into play. In some cases we would expect the representative to be forced by the electoral connection to support a president more than the representative preferred, and in other cases we can see that it may be politically expedient to oppose a president.

The only clear expectation we have is that retirees should, on the whole, change more from one year to the next than do non-retirees. The structure of the situation does not change appreciably for non-retirees, so their support scores in the Congress's second year should approximate their scores in the first year (although certainly we would not expect these scores to be perfectly stable). For the retirees, however, the old constraints are absent and a fairly new kind of situation results. Consequently, I tested the hypothesis using the absolute value of change in presidential support scores. No attention is given to the direction of the change; my only suspicion is that the change in presidential support scores will be greater for retirees than it is for non-retirees.[5] Table 4-7 displays the results of a test of this hypothesis.[6]

Obviously, even those who are not retiring do not maintain pefectly consistent presidential support scores from one year to the next. Some degree of fluctuation would be expected, given the constantly changing political climate and the varying agenda of the House. But we do see from Table 4-7 that on average the change in presidential support scores is greater for retiring members than for those who are running for re-election. Though the overall difference between the two groups is not great (the difference in means of the two columns of numbers is only 1.5), in every Congress save the 90th the group that changed ambition (retired) registered larger absolute changes in presidential support than the group with static ambition (non-retirees). Finding this relationship in nine out of ten elections would occur only one out of one-hundred times by chance. A change in ambition does seem to precipitate some alterations in the tendency of a representative to

Table 4-7

Mean of the Absolute Values of Changes in
Presidential Support Scores From First to
Second Years of Ten Recent Congresses

Congress	Non-retirees	Retirees
86th	9.79	13.67
87th	6.35	10.69
88th	5.48	6.23
89th	4.52	5.02
90th	6.67	4.34
91st	10.83	13.14
92nd	11.92	13.39
93rd	10.60	11.27
94th	8.79	10.64
95th	6.65	8.23

t-value = 1.10; difference in means = 1.50

support or oppose the policies of the incumbent president.

Party Unity Scores

A similar test was performed with party unity scores. These scores are computed by determining the percentage of party votes on which a representative voted in agreement with a majority of his party. (Party votes are defined as those in which a majority of voting Democrats oppose a majority of voting Republicans.) Again, the absolute value of the change is employed since we have no general expectation about the direction of the change, and again our hypothesis is that the mean of the absolute value of the retire's changes in party unity scores will be larger than this same figure for non-retirees. Table 4-8 presents the results of a test of this hypothesis.

Contrary to expectations, being freed from electoral constraints does <u>not</u> seem to encourage retirees to change the degree to which they support their party. Though the mean change for retirees is slightly greater than the mean change for non-retirees (about 1 point greater), careful inspection of Table 4-8 shows that this is largely the result of the 86th and 87th Congresses. In these two Congresses, the change for retirees was quite a bit greater than the change for non-retireses, and if they were removed from the analysis, the overall relationship would no longer be in the expected direction. Even with all Congresses included, in only six of the ten is there a larger change for retirees. All in all, there is little evidence that retirees tend to change their degree of allegiance to party once they decide to retire.

If we had found, as we did in the 86th and 87th Congresses, that upon deciding to retire representatives' party unity scores fluctuated wildly, we would be led to conclude that the party line had been structuring voting behavior when the desire for re-election was present. The fact that such changes are not evident, and the suggestion in the data that they may have occurred in the very early years of this study, seem to be consistent with the widely-held belief that the ability of parties to dispense needed political capital -- money, campaign workers, loyal voters, committee power, and the like -- and thereby help members to get re-elected has lessened.

Table 4-8

Mean of the Absolute Values of Changes in
Party Unity Scores From First to Second
Years of Ten Recent Congresses

Congress	Non-retirees	Retirees
86th	10.88	15.67
87th	7.91	16.66
88th	5.85	4.50
89th	5.69	7.16
90th	6.92	6.63
91st	7.44	3.92
92nd	5.78	3.82
93rd	4.46	5.65
94th	4.18	4.64
95th	3.80	5.84

t-value = .71; difference in means = 1.16

The importance of party relative to individual power bases is said to have decreased, and one interpretation of the findings is that party support scores do not help re-election chances, so there is no need to alter these scores once the desire for re-election is gone.

Basic Ideological Position

A final type of roll call scores I will analyze is the ratings of representatives on various forms of liberal to conservative voting schemes. Two of these voting scales were initially employed: ratings on the Americans for Constitutional Action scale and conservative coalition support scores. Both are obtained by calculating the percentage of the votes cast by a member which are consistent with the positions of the respective groups. In both cases, the higher the score the more conservative the voting behavior of the member.

I later decided to concentrate on the conservative coalition support scores. The "ACA" ratings on a year-by-year basis are not available before 1965. The result for our purposes is that there are usable "ACA" scores in only seven of the ten Congresses of interest. Consequently, I have chosen to utilize the conservative coalition support scores as the measure of ideological position.

The hypothesis is the same as in previous sections. Though for now we will not concern ourselves with the direction in which the retires tend to move, we can reasonable expect that on average their movements will be greater from one year to the next than the movements of non-retirees. This hypothesis is based on the notion that the desire for re-election causes some deviation from a member's preferred course of action -- deviation which becomes unnecessary only when the decision to retire is made. Table 4-9 presents the results of a test of this hypothesis.

There does seem to be some tendency for retirees to alter their basic ideological voting behavior. Conservative coalition support scores are not reported by Congressional Quarterly prior to 1961 so we are left with nine Congresses. In six of these nine, changes in conservative coalition support scores were greater for retirees than for non-retirees. Again, the largest changes seem to occur

Table 4-9

Mean of the Absolute Values of Changes in
Conservative Coalition Support Scores From
First to Second Years of Nine Recent Congresses

Congress	Non-retirees	Retirees
87th	11.60	20.38
88th	10.24	13.55
89th	6.51	7.58
90th	6.92	6.02
91st	6.59	4.70
92nd	6.27	6.51
93rd	5.05	6.28
94th	4.78	4.44
95th	3.95	6.67

t-value = .91; difference in means = 1.56

in the earlier Congresses (especially the 87th). Two of the three cases in which the hypothesis fails involve Congresses from which there were very small numbers of retirees (13 in the 90th and only 8 in the 91st). If we are cautious of any results, it should be those obtained in these two Congresses. Retirees tend to alter their ideological voting position once they decide to retire. In most elections, however, these changes are only slightly greater than the changes registered by non-retirees. Ambition affects behavior in the expected manner, but the size of the effect is not great.

Conclusion

In this chapter I analyzed two consequences of voluntary retirement. The first consequence is that voluntary retirement brings in someone new -- that is, leads to membership turnover. Instead of dealing with the consequences of membership turnover, I focus on the unique type of turnover which results from voluntary retirement. With regard to certain selected characteristics -- partisanship and roll call voting behavior -- successors to retirees tend to be much more similar to the retirees than successors to defeated members are similar to their predecessors. If all turnover in the House resulted from voluntary retirement, my research indicates the expected amount of ideological change would be considerably less than if all turnover resulted from electoral defeat. Though this finding may not be startling, it takes on substantial significance in light of recent changes in the composition of congressional turnover (see Table 4-1).

Perhaps a more subtle consequence of voluntary retirement is that, since most retirement decisions are made at least a year before the end of a term, the retiring representative's behavior may change after the decision to leave. Such a behavioral change is expected because by making the decision to retire the member of Congress removes himself/herself from the sanction of the vote. In effect, the member has disconnected the electoral connection that is supposed to structure a large proportion of congressional behavior. These hypothesized behavioral changes probably do not have a large impact on the public policies produced by Congress since the number of retirees is a small percentage of all members. However, research in this area may be very helpful in providing an understanding of how members of Congress make decisions.

The results of my analysis indicate the decision to retire has a major impact on how often members vote in the House. Participation in roll call votes declined markedly after the need to please voters was removed by the retirement decision. This clarity vanished when attention was shifted from how often members vote to how they vote. There is some indication that members deviate from past behavior more if they decide to retire than if they continue their pattern of running for re-election every two years. This statement is especially true in regard to presidential support scores. On the other hand, removal of electoral constraints does not precipitate much noticeable change in party unity scores.

Taken together, these two findings seem consistent with most descriptions of the current political situation. Representatives have the perception that the public may object to an improper level of presidential support -- either lack of support for a popular president or, more lkely, too much support for an unpopular president. But representatives do not seem to fear public reaction to support for the party that is either too high or too low. Consequently, what behavioral adjustment we see comes in presidential support and not party unity scores. This is not surprising given the more publicized nature of presidential positions relative to party positions.

The decision to retire provides a unique opportunity to study the desire for re-election. My efforts here represent only an admittedly rough first pass through a promising area. By refining efforts to determine the extent and direction of changes precipitated by the choice to leave we can begin to understand how the so-called electoral connection influences the behavior of members of Congress. This information would then be a valuable contribution to the normative questions surrounding the desire to be re-elected -- particularly, does this desire provide the electorate with a needed ability to control the behavior of top officials or does it divert the attention of these officials away from the crucial legislative issues of the day and toward strategies of self-aggrandizement?

Footnotes

[1]See, for example, "Bedell Thinks Congressmen Get Old, Stale, So He Would Limit Terms," *Des Moines Register*, 19 March 1978; and the hearings of the Subcommittee on the Constitution (of the Committee on the Judiciary) of the United States Senate -- 95th Congress -- on S.J. Res. 27 and 28 (March 14 and 16, 1978).

[2]An alternative way of thinking about the situation is to view the election as the stimulus and those who do not choose to run for re-election as the control group. Such a view would certainly be more compatible with Tufte's notion of a political-economic cycle (1978), with politicians changing as the election approaches. But the view employed in this chapter (elections as the norm rather than a stimulus) is consistent with the findings of James Kuklinski in his important article "Representatives and Elections: A Policy Analysis" (1978). Kuklinski finds that legislators who have only two-year terms do not have the opportunity to relax in the off-year. The term is so short that every year in effect becomes an election year. As a result, elections are always on the minds of these legislators, unless of course they are retiring.

[3]According to some, tests of significance are not needed in this situation because we do not have a sample of legislators, but instead have the entire population of legislators who served in the House in the last ten Congresses. Nonetheless, it is useful to know how likely it is that the differences in the two columns of numbers appearing in Table 4-6 occurred by chance. To obtain a test of significance, I ran a regression equation with the two columns of numbers as the dependent variable. The independent variable was a dummy variable with zero (0) coded for means of non-retirees and one (1) coded for means of retirees. The t-value displayed here is the t-value for the slope of the coefficient for the dummy variable. The slope itself is the difference in means of the two columns. A similar procedure was performed for Tables 4-7, 4-8, and 4-9.

[4]As computed by Congressional Quarterly, presidential support scores are influenced by attendance levels. Failure to vote lowers support scores. In light of the findings of the previous

section, a serious bias could be introduced into the scores by differential participation levels. To control for this problem, presidential support scores for each individual are divided by the sum of that member's presidential support and presidential opposition. Thus, someone whose presidential support score was 40 and opposition was 20 would get a corrected presidential support score of 67. This same procedure was used to correct party unity scores and conservative coalition support scores since they, too, are influenced by attendance levels.

[5]An analysis of the direction of the changes proved inconclusive when conducted with presidential support scores and party unity scores. A discussion of the direction of changes in conservative coalition support is undertaken elsewhere (Hibbing, 1980:142-144).

[6]The number of cases is not presented in this and subsequent tables because in each category the "N" will be the same as that given in the parentheses of Table 4-6.

CHAPTER 5

CONCLUSION: THE CASE OF THE VANISHING INCUMBENTS

This study was spurred by the sharp increase in the number of voluntary retirements from the House which occurred in the 1970s, but I quickly found that to analyze this phenomenon properly it is essential to come to grips with the more general issues of political ambitions and motivations. Thus I have concentrated on why members retire rather than on why so many more retired in the 1970s than in the 1960s. I have focused on the general consequences of people leaving voluntarily rather than on the consequences of the recent increase in retirements. But now we are in a position to complete the circle by returning to the original stimulus of this research. Why did the number of retirees go up and what are the results of this increase?

Three different ways of exploring the causes of voluntary retirement were employed in this work -- aggregate time-series analyses, personal interviews with recent retirees, and a cross-sectional analysis of the traits which predispose some members to retire or, conversely, encourages members to stay. The most successful variable in each method of inquiry was what I call the seniority variable. In the time-series data, the existence of a religiously applied seniority rule to select committee and subcommittee chairmen correlates quite highly with low numbers of retirements. The sure payoff which the seniority rule supplies those who stay in the House for extended careers encourages them to do just that. When this security is absent (as it was in the very early 1900s and in the 1970s) increased numbers of members retire voluntarily. In the interviews I conducted I heard an extraordinary amount of criticism of the "reforms" in the seniority system although, as is evident from Chapter 2, critical comments about the modern Congress certainly were not limited to the demise of seniority. Finally, the cross-sectional analysis reported in Chapter 3 indicates most clearly the power of the seniority variable. Seniority was the most potent predictor of retirement in the 1970s because it had been devalued by the changes in the system. Further, the timing of changes in the ability of the seniority variable to predict retirement is perfectly consistent with the actual changes in the seniority system. Finally, senior Democrats, as expected, are affected the most by the changes.

The procedures by which powerful committee positions are allocated have a tremendous impact on how members plan for and engage in long-term careers. In light of this research, the desire to maximize power within the House certainly deserves the place Fenno accords it as one of the three prime motivations of members of Congress (1973:3) and may deserve the place it is granted by Jones and Woll as the major motivation of representatives (1979).

I believe that in addition to receiving support from the diverse modes of data employed here, an emphasis on the ability of changes in the seniority system to explain the increase in voluntary retirements is appealing on a common sense basis. It does not require a revision of the traditional wisdom regarding political ambition. This traditional view is that politicians want to acquire more power than they currently hold, and we see now that despite a high rate of voluntary retirement, this is still the case. The problem is that with an uncertain method of distributing power positions the acquisition of additional power as one moves through a career may not happen, and power already possessed may even be taken away. Faced with this situation representatives decide they would rather not play at all than play with new, and to some extent undefined, rules. Members of Congress have not suddenly become less ambitious. They are doing what they have always done: making calculatiions about future situations from information available at present. This is the basis of ambition theory and it is still as applicable as ever. The change is that now the results of these calculations are different than they used to be. At times they indicate getting out may be better than leaving one's future in the hands of a caucus whose decisions at times seem to be fairly arbitrary. For example, several members told me the reason W.R. Poage was removed as chairman of the Agriculture Committee in the 1975 coups was that his committee comes first in the alphabet and therefore was the first for which the caucus voted on a chairman. The theory is that after the caucus had "drawn blood" it relaxed more and more as the committees further down the alphabet were voted upon. Though this explanation is somewhat questionable, it illustrates the belief of many members about how highly capricious the caucus' decisions can be. (It is also interesting to note that the other committees to have chairmen deposed in 1975 -- Armed Services and Banking -- come quite early in the alphabet.)

To be sure, it would be overly simplistic to maintain there is only one cause of the 1970s increase in voluntary retirements. Seniority is important but it is not the sole cause, and at several points in this study I discuss some of these other variables. The low salary (relative to executive and professional salaries in the private sector) certainly is an important consideration for many members. If there is no salary increase in the 98th Congress and if inflation does not cease altogether, the real salary of members of Congress in 1983 will be at its lowest level in 25 years. The importance of salary considerations should not be ignored, as is evident from the statements of former members as well as the time-series correlation of salary and the number of retirements.

Several other variables also come to mind and many of these have been addressed in past research and in earlier pages of this study -- especially the section describing the results of my interviews. I am convinced members are disaffected with some parts of modern congressional service. This is important in itself. However, the connection of this disaffection to the increase in voluntary retirements is somewhat troublesome. First, it needs to be shown that this disaffection increased in the 1970s after decreasing through the 1950s and 1960s. I know of no evidence which indicates the level of disaffection in the 1970s was higher than in the 1960s. It may be that, if they had been asked, retirees in the 1960s would have voiced complaints, gripes, and criticisms similar to those voiced in Chapter 2 by those who retired in 1978. Many of those who believe disaffection has increased use the higher retirement rate as evidence, thus completing the following airtight and wholly nonsensical circle. More disaffection causes more retirements. How do we know there is more disaffection? We know because there are more voluntary retirements.

Even if we assume disaffection has grown, the timing of the change must match the timing of the increase in voluntary retirements. Many of the presumed elements of the increased disaffection do not meet this criterion. The hectic pace has evolved gradually, disrespect for politicians has grown gradually, the size of the bureaucracy and the associated amount of casework has grown slowly, the media exposure has increased gradually, and the abrasive new type of member has entered Congress a few at a time. None of these changes comes close to matching the abrupt increase in retirements which occurred in 1972 and the subsequent leveling off in the rest of the 1970s (see Table 1-1). The growth in the number of retirees has been anything but slow and steady, thus it fits poorly with many widely accepted explanations. If we do attempt to assign specific dates to some of the sources of disaffection, these dates still do not mesh with the increase in retirements. Watergate may be responsible for the decreased respect for politicians, but why did the increase in retirements come before Watergate was made into a major issue? The 1975 entering class may have been particularly contentious, but why did the increase in retirements come years before this class ever entered the House? Furthermore, until the 1970s the retirement rate was dropping at the same time all these alleged components of disaffection were growing. This situation more than any other casts doubt on the disaffection argument. We should not uncritically accept an explanation such as disaffection on the basis of simplistic appeal. I am not suggesting it is wrong, only that it is unproven, incomplete, and so broad and vague as to be meaningless. By focusing on particular aspects of congressional service and by analyzing the timing of the change in retirement rates as well as the particular groups which should be most affected by the change, we are able to gain more specific and useful information on the causes of voluntary retirement. When this is done we are forced to return to the seniority explanation. Changes in the seniority rule were first made in 1971. The first opportunity to leave after the changes was in 1972, and this is precisely when the increase in retirements arrived. Thus an emphasis on seniority, without going so far as to rule out the supplemental impact of other factors, seems to constitute the most sensible conclusion regarding the causes of the increase in retirements.

Voluntary retirements from Congress lose much of their significance as a topic of study if no attention is given to their consequences. Thus in Chapter 4 I turn to two of these consequences. One consequence is the behavioral change which results from the decision to retire. In a representative democracy the desire to please the voters and thereby be returned to office provides the crucial nexus between voters and elected officials. The situation is altered fundamentally when the decision to retire severs this connection. As a result, this particular consequence of voluntary retirement may be more valuable for our understanding of congressional decision-making than for any direct link to the type of policy passed by Congress in any one year. A second consequence is turnover. It is fairly easy to demonstrate that, in terms of partisanship and ideology, voluntary retirement is a type of turnover which brings less change than does electoral defeat. This much is consistent with past research. But as noted at the end of Chapter 3, this is only part of the story. If we look beyond roll call scores and party identification, voluntary retirement may bring more change than electoral defeat -- particularly in areas such as the amount of experience and legislative savvy. Though this statement is probably applicable to voluntary retirement in all time periods, it is especially true of the 1970s when large numbers of very senior people chose to leave. One clear consequence of the recent increase in voluntary retirements is the loss of numerous experienced legislators.

Whether or not this loss is compensated by the growth in the number of young members, who are presumably vigorous and full of new ideas, is a judgment matter. The optimal amount of turnover for a legislative body is an open question. Certainly it is not difficult to see the dangers of both too little and too much turnover. But beyond this, conclusions regarding the best level of turnover depend upon how comfortable we are with the status quo and upon our own views of the type of legislature we want. Depending upon how we view these issues, the growth in the rate of voluntary retirement may have provided a needed influx of new, untainted members into a previously closed and stuffy body or it may have led to a devastating loss of legislative expertise and an equally harmful increase in self-centered and legislatively unskilled new members.

REFERENCES

Abramson, Rudy. "Up-and-Coming Congressman Quits." Los Angeles Times, 3 August 1980, sec. 8, pp. 2-3.

Alford, John R. and John R. Hibbing. "Increased Incumbency Advantage in the House." Journal of Politics, 43 (November 1981): 1042-1061.

Asher, Herbert B., and Weisberg, Herbert, F. "Congressional Voting Change: A Longitudinal Study of Voting on Selected Issues." Paper presented at the 1975 Annual Meeting of the American Political Science Association, San Francisco, California, 1975.

Barber, James David. The Lawmakers. New Haven: Yale University Press, 1965.

Best, Fred. "A History of the Linear Life Plan and Its Alternatives." Paper prepared for the Secretary of Education, United States Department of Health, Education and Welfare. Washington, D.C., 1976. (Mimeographed.)

Bethel, Tom. "The Disadvantaged Congress." Harper's, April 1979, pp. 24-28.

Biographical Directory of the American Congress, 1774-1971. Washington, D.C.: U.S. Government Printing Office, 1971.

Black, Gordon. "A Theory of Political Ambition." American Political Science Review 66 (March 1972):144-159.

Bluedorn, Allen C. "A Taxonomy of Turnover." The Pennsylvania State University, 1978. (Mimeographed.)

Bogue, Allen; Clubb, Jerome M.; McKibben, Carroll L.; and Traugott, Santa A. "Members of the House of Representatives and the Process of Modernization, 1789-1960." Journal of American History 63 (September 1976):275-302.

Buchanon, Christopher. "Congressional Retirements Drop in 1980." Congressional Quarterly Weekly Report, 12 January 1980, pp. 79-82.

Bullock, Charles S. "House Careerists: Changing Patterns of Longevity and Attrition." American Political Science Review 66 (December 1972):- 1295-1300.

Congressional Quarterly. Representation and Apportionment. Washington, D.C.: Congressional Quarterly, Inc., 1966.

_____. Congressional Ethics. Washington, D.C.: Congressional Quarterly, Inc., 1977.

_____. Inside Congress. Washington, D.C.: Congressional Quarterly, Inc., 1979.

_____. Weekly Report. Washington, D.C.: Congressional Quarterly, Inc., 1979.

Cooper, Joseph and William West. "The Congressional Career in the 1970s." In Lawrence C. Dodd and Bruce I. Oppenheimer, eds., Congress Reconsidered (second edition), pp. 83-106, Washington, D.C.: Congressional Quarterly, 1981a.

_____. "Voluntary Retirement, Incumbency, and the Moderen House." Political Science Quarterly 96 (Summer 1981b): 279-300.

Cover, Albert D. "The Greening of Congress: Patterns of Voluntary Retirement." Paper prepared for delivery at the annual meeting of the Midwest Political Science Association, Cincinnati, Ohio, April, 1981.

Deckard, Barbara. "State Party Delegations in the U.S. House of Representatives." Journal of Politics 34 (February 1972):199-222.

Des Moines Register. "Jimmy Carter's Sacrifice." 4 May 1980, p. Cl.

Dodd, Lawrence C. "Congress and the Quest for Power." In Lawrence C. Dodd and Bruce I. Oppenheimer, eds., Congress Reconsidered, pp. 269-307. New York: Praeger, 1977.

Dodd, Lawrence C., and Bruce I. Oppenheimer. The House in Transition: Change and Consolidation. In Lawrence C. Dodd and Bruce I. Oppenheimer, eds., Congress Reconsidered (second edition), pp. 31-61. Washington, D.C.: Congressional Quarterly, 1981.

Eulau, Heinz, and Sprague, John D. Lawyers in Politics. Indianapolis: Bobb-Merrill, 1964.

Fenno, Richard F. Congressmen in Committees. Boston: Little, Brown and Co., 1973.

_____. "If, as Ralph Nader Says, Congress is a Broken Branch, How Come We Love Our Congressmen So Much?" In Congress in Change, pp. 277-287. Edited by Norman J. Ornstein. New York: Praeger, 1975.

_____. Home Style. Boston: Little, Brown and Co., 1978.

Fiorina, Morris P.; Rohde, David W.; and Wissel, Peter. "Historical Change in House Turnover." In Congress in Change, pp. 24-57. Edited by Norman J. Ornstein. New York: Praeger, 1975.

Fiorina, Morris P. Congress: Keystone to the Washington Establishment. New Haven: Yale University Press, 1977.

Fishel, Jeff. "Ambition and the Political Vocation." Journal of Politics 33 (February 1971):25-56.

_____. Party and Opposition. New York: David McKay, 1973.

Frantzich, Stephen E. "De-Recruitment: The Other Side of the Congressional Equation." Western Political Quarterly 31 (March 1978):105-126.

_____. "Opting Out: Retirement from the House of Representatives." American Politics Quarterly 6 (July 1978):251-273.

Frost, Murray. "Senatorial Ambition and Legislative Behavior." Ph.D. dissertation, Michigan State University, 1972.

Galloway, George B. History of the House of Representatives. 2nd Edition. Revised by Sidney Wise. New York: Crowell, 1976.

Gillespie, Michael W. "Log-Linear Techniques and the Regression Analysis of Dummy Dependent Variables." Sociological Methods and Research 6 (August 1977):103-122.

Hain, Paul. "Age, Ambition and Political Careers." Western Political Quarterly 27 (June 1974):265--274.

Hibbing, John R. "Retired From the House: The Causes and Consequences of Voluntary Retirement." Ph.D. dissertation, University of Iowa, 1980.

_____. "Voluntary Retirement From the House: The Costs of Congressional Service." Legislative Studies Quarterly 7 (February 1982a): in press.

_____. "Voluntary Retirement from the U.S. House of Representatives: Who Quits?" American Journal of Political Science, 26 (August 1982b): forthcoming.

Hinckley, Barbara. "Seniority 1975: Old Theories Confront New Facts." British Journal of Political Science 6 (October 1976):383-399.

Huntington, Samuel P. "Congressional Responses to the Twentieth Century." In Congress and America's Future, pp. 5-31. Edited by David B. Truman. Englewood Cliffs, New Jersey: Prentice-Hall, 1965.

Hyde, John. "Bedell Thinks Congressmen Get Old, Stale, So He Would Limit Terms." Des Moines Register, 19 March 1978, p. 10.

Hyneman, Charles. "Tenure and Turnover in Legislative Personnel." Annals of the American Academy of Political and Social Science 195 (January 1938):21-31.

Jewell, Malcolm. "Attitudinal Determinants of Legislative Behavior." In Legislatures in Developmental Perspective, pp. 460-500. Edited by Alan Kornberg and Lloyd Musolf. Durham: Duke University Press, 1970.

Jewell, Malcolm, and Patterson, Samuel C. The Legislative Process in the United States. New York: Random House, 1977.

Johnson, Kathryn. "Why So Many Lawmakers Are Calling It Quits." U.S. News and World Report, 25 August 1980, pp. 43-44.

Jones, Charles O. "Inter-Party Competition for Congressional Seats." Western Political Quarterly 17 (September 1964):461-476.

_____. "Will Reform Change Congress?" In Lawrence C. Dodd and Bruce I. Oppenheimer, eds., Congress Rconsidered, pp.247-260. New York: Praeger, 1977.

_____. "New Directions In U.S. Congressional Research." Legislative Studies Quarterly 6 (August 1981):455-468.

Jones, Rochelle, and Peter Woll. The Private World of Congress. New York: Free Press, 1979.

Kent, Frank. The Great Game of Politics. New York: Doubleday, 1936.

Klecka, William R. Discriminant Analysis. Beverly Hills, California: Sage Publications, Inc., 1980.

Kmenta, Jan. Elements of Econometrics. New York: MacMillan, 1971.

Kort, Fred. "Regression Analysis and Discriminant Analysis: An Application of R.A. Fisher's Theorem to Data in Political Science. American Political Science Review 67 (June 1973):555-559.

Kritzer, Herbert M. "The Senatorial Ambitions of U.S. Representatives: The Decision to Run." Paper presented at the 1978 Annual Meeting of the Southern Political Science Association, Atlanta, Georgia, 9-11 November 1978.

Kuklinski, James H. "Representatives and Elections: A Policy Analysis." American Political Science Review 72 (March 1978):165-177.

Laswell, Harold. <u>Power and Personality</u>. Stanford: Stanford University Press, 1948.

Lerner, Daniel; Laswell, Harold; and Rothwell, C. Easton. <u>The Comparative Study of Elites</u>. Stanford: Stanford University Press, 1951.

Mann, Thomas E. <u>Unsafe At Any Margin</u>. Washington: American Enterprise Institute, 1978.

Mayhew, David R. "Congressional Elections: The Case of the Vanishing Marginals." <u>Polity</u> 6 (Spring 1974a):295-317.

_____. <u>Congress: The Electoral Connection</u>. New Haven: Yale University Press, 1974b.

Mezey, Michael. "Ambition Theory." <u>Journal of Politics</u> 32 (August 1970):563-579.

O'Brien, Patricia. "No Honor After Watergate: Congressmen Quit." <u>Des Moines Register</u>, 5 March 1978, p. 1.

Pindyck, R.S., and Rubinfeld, D.L. <u>Econometric Models and Economic Forecasts</u>. New York: McGraw-Hill, 1976.

Polsby, Nelson W. "The Institutionalization of the House of Representatives." <u>American Political Science Review</u> 62 (March 1968):144-168.

Polsby, Nelson W.; Gallaher, Miriam; and Rundquist, Barry. "The Growth of the Seniority System in the U.S. House of Representatives." <u>American Political Science Review</u> 63 (September 1969):-787-807.

Prewitt, Kenneth, and Nowlin, William. "Political Ambitions and the Behavior of Incumbent Politicians." <u>Western Political Quarterly</u> 22 (June 1969):298-308.

Prewitt, Kenneth, and Eulau, Heinz. "Political Matrix and Political Representation." <u>American Political Science Review</u> 63 (June 1969): 427-441.

Prewitt, Kenneth. "Political Ambitions, Volunteerism, and Electoral Accountability." <u>American Political Science Review</u> 64 (March 1970):5-17.

Price, H. Douglas. "The Congressional Career: Then and Now." In Congressional Behavior, pp. 14-27. Edited by Nelson Polsby. New York: Random House, 1971.

_____. "Congress and the Evolution of Legislative Professionalism." In Congress in Change, pp. 2-23. Edited by Norman J. Ornstein. New York: Praeger, 1975.

_____. "Careers and Committees in the American Congress." In The History of Parliamentary Behavior, pp. 28-62. Edited by William O. Aydelotte. Princeton: Princeton University Press, 1977.

Ray, David. "Voluntary Retirement and Electoral Defeat in Eight State Legislatures." Journal of Politics 38 (May 1976):426-433.

Rowen, Hobart. "Reagan or Carter, Little Difference on Economics." Des Moines Register, 4 May 1980, p. C2.

Rohde, David W. "Risk-Bearing and Progressive Ambition: The Case of Members of the United States House of Representatives." American Journal of Political Science 23 (February 1979):1-26.

Rhodes, John JU. The Futile System. MacLean, Virginia: EPM, 1976.

Schlesinger, Joseph A. Ambition and Politics. Chicago: Rand McNally, 1966.

Sekscenski, Edward S. "Job Tenure Declines as Work Force Changes." Monthly Labor Review, December 1979, pp. 48-50.

Sinclair, Ward. "Grazing in the Tall Grass of Retirement," Washington Post, 18 January 1980, p. 1.

Soule, John W. "Fugure Political Ambitions and the Behavioir of Incumbent State Legislators." Midwest Journal of Political Science 13 (August 1969):439-454.

Stone, Pauline Terrelonge. "Ambition Theory and the Black Politician." Western Political Quarterly 33 (March 1980):94-107.

Struble, Robert. "House Turnover and the Principle of Rotation." <u>Political Science Quarterly</u> 94 (Winter 1979-80):649-667.

Swinerton, E. Nelson. "Ambition and American State Executives." <u>Midwestern Journal of Political Science</u> 12 (November 1968):538-549.

Tufte, Edward R. <u>Political Control of the Economy</u>. Princeton: Princeton University Press, 1978.

U.S. Congress. Senate. Committee on the Judiciary. Hearings before the Subcommittee on the Constitution on S.J. 27 and S.J. 28, 95th Congress, 2nd session, March 14 and 16, 1978. Washington, D.C.: U.S. Government Printing Office, 1978.

U.S. Department of Commerce. Bureau of the Census. <u>Historical Statistics</u>. Bicentennial Edition. Washington, D.C.: U.S.Government Printing Office, 1976.

Van der Silk, Jack, and Pernaciarrio, Samuel. "Office Ambitions and Voting Behavior in the U.S. Senate." <u>American Politics Quarterly</u> 7 (April 1979).

Wittmer, T. Richard. "The Aging of the House." <u>Political Science Quarterly</u> 79 (December 1964):526-541.

Walters, Robert. "How Some Congressmen Tap Extra Funds." <u>Parade</u>, 24 August 1975.

ABOUT THE AUTHOR

John R. Hibbing was raised on a farm near Paullina, Iowa. He received his B.S. from Dana College in Blair, Nebraska, before attending the University of Iowa where he received his M.A. and, in 1980, his Ph.D. in political science. Hibbing has taught at Oakland University and at the University of Nebraska-Lincoln where he is currently assistant professor in the Department of Political Science. His research interests include congressional elections and congressional careers as well as the interaction of Congress and the executive branch -- particularly the independent regulatory commissions. His articles have appeared in the American Journal of Political Science, the British Journal of Political Science, the Journal of Politics, and the Legislative Studies Quarterly. He is married to Anne Nielsen and they have one child, Michael, age 1.